Edited by John Foster

MACMILLAN ENGLISH

Talking and Writing from Experience

JUDITH ATKINSON &

JOHN FOSTER

MACMILLAN

First edition 1991

Published by
MACMILLAN EDUCATION LTD
Houndmills, Basingstoke, Hampshire RG21 2XS
and London
Companies and representatives
throughout the world

Printed in Hong Kong

British Library Cataloguing in Publication Data
Atkinson, Judith
Talking and writing from experience.—(Macmillan English)
I. Title II. Foster, John
428

ISBN 0–333–52538–8

ACKNOWLEDGEMENTS

The authors and publishers wish to thank the following who have kindly given permission for the use of copyright material.

Moira Andrew for 'The day I caught chickenpox' Carcanet Press Ltd. for 'The Artist' from *Collected Poems* by William Carlos Williams; Carel Press for 'A Ghoul' by Naomi Green from *Away from Home*, edited by Chas White and Christine Shepherd. Copyright © Carel Press; Collins Publishers for 'Midnight' ('Caught in the act') by Neil McIntosh from *Kid's Stuff*, compiled by Wendy Craig; English Centre for extracts from 'Small Accidents' by Sabir Bandali from *Our Lives* and 'Margaret's Story' from *Many Lives*, ILEA; Eric Finney for 'Progress Report'; David Lodge for 'The Miser' from *Kid's Stuff*, compiled by Wendy Craig, Collins Publishers; Macmillan Publishers Ltd. for material from *Appropriate English* by Adams, Foster et al. and 'The Cheetah and the Rollerskate' by Sasha Norton from *Words in Action* by Bruce Jameson and John Foster; Random Century Group for an extract from *The Frog Report* by Benjamin Lee, Hutchinson; Rogers, Coleridge & White Ltd. for an extract from *Lay By* by Gareth Owen; Syndication International Ltd. for an extract from 'Mother shelling peas' by Katherine Board from *Children as Writers*, the 10th Daily Mirror Children's Literary Competition; Thorsons for an extract from 'Gran' by Valerie Avery from *London Morning*, William Kimber.

Every effort has been made to trace all copyright holders, but if any have been inadvertently overlooked the publishers will be pleased to make the necessary arrangement at the first opportunity.

Editorial coordination by
   Gill Stacey and Liz Paren
Text design by Susan Clarke
Cover design by Quadraphic
Illustrations by Linda Combi,
Frank Nichols, Ursula Sieger,
Chris Williams

CONTENTS

INTRODUCTION

The Talking and writing from experience module in the *Macmillan English* series is a flexible resource of eight substantial assignments. Its aim is to develop students' ability to describe their personal experiences and to express their ideas, thoughts and feelings in a range of different written forms.

The assignments and suggested tasks are directly related to the National Curriculum attainment targets and programmes of study for Key Stage 3:

'Pupils should have opportunities to
- write in a range of forms, including the following: notes, diaries, personal letters, chronological accounts, pamphlets, book reviews, advertisements, comic strips, poems, stories, playscripts
- write for a range of purposes including describing, explaining, giving instructions, reporting, expressing a point of view
- organise and express their meaning appropriately for different specified audiences.'

> *Programme of study for writing: General provisions for Key Stage 3 (Paragraph 25)*

The assignments contain a range of lively and interesting materials, selected not only because they provide models for analysis and discussion, but also because they are intrinsically interesting and enjoyable to read. They range from Moira Andrew's diary account of a day spent at home suffering from chicken pox and David Lodge's story *The Miser* about a childhood disappointment, to teenagers' own accounts of their earliest memories and reflections on their relationships with other members of their families. The tasks invite the students to explore and analyse the different pieces of writing through pair and group discussion activities, and then to put into practice the techniques they have observed by writing in a particular form for a specified audience.

The assignments and tasks suggested here encourage a holistic approach to reading, speaking and listening and writing. A consequence of this is that the possible language outcomes are enormous and the tasks are likely to generate responses across the entire Key Stage 3 range of attainment levels from 3 to 8. This should not be seen as a problem, but rather as an opportunity to guide and develop achievement to the maximum.

In relation to assessment it is important that the statements and levels of attainment set out in the statutory orders inform rather than overwhelm judgement and good practice. For such a complex act as writing, there can be no easy relationship between the processes of developing and communicating meaning in a particular form for a specific audience and purpose and a figure on a ten-point scale. The gradual growth of writing sophistication cannot be characterised as the simple acquisition of additional skills, whilst moving on a linear track. The processes of speaking and listening and of reading are similarly complex and equally difficult to plot on a scale. In both cases, the level of sophistication a student achieves will vary according to the task and its context.

Assessment needs, therefore, to be made over an extended period of time, during which the teacher builds up a picture of the student's performance, rather than by compiling a checklist after the completion of each task. Further suggestions for recording and assessment are made on Sheets 67–68.

It is useful to clarify the criteria used to link the assignments and tasks to the detailed requirements of the statements of attainment.

The assignments and tasks suggested here enable students to

1 *Read and discuss personal writing with understanding* by
- talking about a range of styles of writing, giving evidence of personal response
- developing their own insights and sustaining them by reference to the text
- showing an understanding of the author's approach, depending on the form, the purpose and the audience

2 *Develop the ability to describe personal experiences, thoughts and emotions* by
- developing narrative accounts of personal experiences
- giving explanations and information about personal interests
- expressing opinions and developing arguments and points of view
- listening and responding to the experiences and viewpoints of others in pair and group discussions

3 *Understand and practise the techniques writers use in personal writing* by
- understanding that the writing process involves several stages from collecting ideas through to presentation
- structuring and organising pieces of writing according to purpose and audience
- understanding how to choose the style and language that is appropriate to the form, the purpose and the audience
- writing in a wide variety of forms, including the following: autobiographical accounts, descriptions, explanations, poems, stories, diaries, letters

This list is not exhaustive and opportunities remain for teachers and students to develop fresh approaches of their own.

(For teachers who would welcome a sifting and sorting of those statements of attainment most directly addressed in this module see Sheets 69–70.)

Judith Atkinson
John Foster

THE ASSIGNMENTS

Throughout this module there are frequent suggestions and opportunities for drafting and redrafting writing, both individually and in consultation with others. Apart from Assignment 8, no specific reference is made to drafting on word processors. However, it is presumed that wherever facilities are available students will be encouraged to make full use of them and to learn the skills of drafting on a computer screen as well as on paper.

ASSIGNMENT 1 TELLING STORIES – THIS IS MY LIFE

Aim To look at some of the different ways we can tell people about our lives and to write a number of short autobiographical pieces

TASK 1 **My earliest days 1** presents three examples in which people write about their earliest memories. Students are asked to assemble their own ideas, then to write the first draft of an autobiographical account 'My earliest days' for readers of their own age.
Suitable for attainment levels 3–7 in all three profile components.

TASK 2 **My earliest days 2** is a redrafting exercise. Students work in pairs to make suggestions about how to develop the first draft by a pupil called Waseem, before offering each other advice on how to redraft their own pieces.

Suitable for attainment levels 3–7 in writing.

TASK 3 **A day like any other** Students are asked to prepare a piece of writing in which they tell a reader what their lives are like by focusing upon four moments in a typical day.
Suitable for attainment levels 3–7 in writing.

TASK 4 **Family scenes** A scene from a Gareth Owen play is used to show how an everyday family scene can be presented in the form of a playscript. There are suggestions for tape-recording and/or developing the scene, for role-plays and for writing and recording their own radio scripts.
Suitable for attainment levels 3–7 in all three profile components.

ASSIGNMENT 2 DESCRIBING PEOPLE

Aim To explore ways of describing people that convey to the reader not only what they look like but also what sort of characters they have

TASK 1 **Pen portraits** Advice on how to construct convincing pen portraits is given in the form of an extract from Benjamin Lee's novel *The Frog Report*. The emphasis is on choosing details selectively and on keeping the character sketches short and pithy.
Suitable for attainment levels 3–7 in all three profile components.

TASK 2 **Snapshot poems** presents three poems, all of which describe people in action through close observation – William Carlos Williams's *The artist*, Katherine Board's *Mother shelling peas* and Ian Griffiths' *The penknife glides*. Students are then asked to build up their own poems based on the close observation of a person in action.
Suitable for attainment levels 3–7 in all three profile components.

TASK 3 **A detailed description** aims to get students to write a detailed description of a person, creating a clear impression of her/him by describing the person's character and habits as well as her/his appearance. Valerie Avery's description of her grandmother is presented as a model for them to analyse and imitate.
Suitable for attainment levels 3–8 in all three profile components.

TASK 4 **A life story through interview** offers an alternative approach to character description, suggesting that the students start by interviewing a person, then use what the person tells them as the basis for writing a part of her/his life story. Extracts from a girl's interview with her grandmother about life during the second world war are provided to show how the task can be tackled.
Suitable for attainment levels 3–8 in speaking and listening and writing.

ASSIGNMENT 3 DESCRIBING PLACES

Aim To practise writing descriptions of places for a number of different purposes

TASK 1 **My neighbourhood** provides a description of an 'enchanted alley' by Michael Anthony as an example of how to capture the atmosphere of a place. Students are then asked to draft pieces of writing which capture the atmosphere of some places they know well.
Suitable for attainment levels 3–7 in all three profile components.

TASK 2 **A perfect place to live** Students have to design an ideal home and produce a

detailed piece of factual writing describing it.
Suitable for attainment levels 3–8 in writing.

TASK 3 **A place I'll always remember** After discussing a description by Dirk Bogarde of a place where he and his sister often played as children, students have to plan, draft and write a detailed description of a place they remember clearly for some reason.
Suitable for attainment levels 3–8 in all three profile components.

ASSIGNMENT 4 INFORMING AND EXPLAINING

Aim To practise ways of talking and writing about your personal interests and of explaining the customs and celebrations which are part of your life

TASK 1 **My interests 1** involves the preparation and presentation of a talk on a subject in which the speaker is interested, but which may be unfamiliar to the audience.
Suitable for attainment levels 3–8 in speaking and listening.

TASK 2 **My interests 2** Students are asked to write an article for people of their own age about a hobby or sport in which they

are interested. An article by a teenager called Joelle, describing how she took up water-skiing, is presented as a model.
Suitable for attainment levels 3–8 in writing.

TASK 3 **Customs and celebrations** involves students in writing for a specified audience about the customs and celebrations that form a part of their lives. Articles by two teenagers about Diwali and Ramadan are presented for reading and discussion.
Suitable for levels 3–8 in all three profile components.

ASSIGNMENT 5 TELLING STORIES – A MOMENT TO REMEMBER

Aim To examine and practise some of the techniques that can be used when writing narrative accounts of personal experiences

TASK 1 **First person narrative** After discussing Neil Mackintosh's account of a childhood escapade, students are asked to share similar experiences in a group discussion before writing their own first person narratives.
Suitable for attainment levels 3–8 in all three profile components.

TASK 2 **First and third person narrative 1** After reading a short story, *The cheetah and the rollerskate*, which Sasha Norton wrote when she was a teenager, students in pairs

are asked to think about the first and third person narratives and to draft two different versions of a story.
Suitable for attainment levels 3–8 in all three profile components.

TASK 3 **First and third person narrative 2** David Lodge's story *The miser* is presented and students are asked to discuss its content, structure and style before writing their own stories based on a personal experience of a disappointment or a surprise, using either the first person or the third person.
Suitable for attainment levels 3–8 in all three profile components.

ASSIGNMENT 6 DESCRIBING AND REFLECTING

Aim To write in a variety of forms – diaries, essays and journals – describing and reflecting upon personal experiences

TASK 1 **Diary writing** After reading and discussing extracts from a diary in which

Moira Andrew describes having to stay in bed with chickenpox, students are asked to write their own diary entries in an appropriate style.
Suitable for attainment levels 3–8 in all three profile components.

TASK 2 **Reflective writing** presents two examples in which Maria, aged fourteen, and Tariq, aged fifteen, write about their families and reflect upon their relationships within the family. Students are then asked to write reflectively about their own home lives and relationships.

Suitable for attainments levels 3–8 in all three profile components.

TASK 3 **A reading journal** explores three different approaches to keeping a reading journal – keeping a journal while reading, responding to a book after reading it and reviewing responses to a book in an interview and then recording the responses in a journal. Students are then asked to keep a reading journal of their own.

Suitable for attainment levels 3–8 in all three profile components.

ASSIGNMENT 7 LETTERS

Aim To practise writing different types of personal letters, conveying information and opinions

TASK I **Letter to a penfriend** presents students with an example of an introductory letter to a new penfriend and then asks them to choose a penfriend from a page of advertisements and to write their own letters of introduction.

Suitable for attainment levels 3–8 in writing.

TASK 2 **Letters giving information** asks students to write letters in which they give a

person clear instructions about how to get somewhere.

Suitable for attainment levels 3–8 in writing.

TASK 3 **In my opinion** Working in groups, students have to read six letters from *The Indy* and choose one of them as the week's star letter. After comparing the techniques the six writers use, students are then asked to draft their own letters on issues of concern to them.

Suitable for attainment levels 3–8 in all three profile components.

ASSIGNMENT 8 SCHOOL – THE INSIDE STORY

Aim This assignment offers the opportunity for students to practise the skills they have been developing throughout the module by writing for a variety of different purposes – to describe, to tell stories, to inform and to explain. The aim is for groups of students to work together to produce a booklet for new pupils telling them 'the inside story of life at your school'

TASK I **Describing places and scenes** asks students to think about places and scenes in their school and to choose an appropriate way of describing them.

Suitable for attainment levels 3–8 in writing.

TASK 2 **Describing experiences** After reading and discussing a detailed account of an art project which the writer, Naomi, found memorable, students are invited to share memories of events they have experienced at school and then to write their own accounts of memorable incidents.

Suitable for attainment levels 3–8 in all three profile components.

TASK 3 **Explaining and informing** involves conveying information in a clear and appropriate way for a specific audience. Students are asked to select the best way of providing essential information for a pupil who is about to start at their school.

Suitable for attainment levels 3–8 in writing.

TASK 4 **The 'inside' story** The aim is for students to write about the 'things that teachers won't tell you about your new school' choosing an appropriate form and style in order to make the writing as entertaining as possible.

Suitable for attainment levels 3–8 in writing.

TASK 5 **Writing up the booklet** Working in groups, the students are asked to collect together the pieces they have written in the previous four tasks in this assignment and to design and produce their booklet for new pupils. There are lots of possibilities for using word processors for this work, depending, of course, on availability.

Suitable for attainment levels 3–8 in speaking and listening and writing.

My earliest days 1

Aim To research and write the first draft of an autobiographical account of 'My earliest days' for readers of your own age

Here are three people writing about their earliest memories:

I will begin to tell you about my life, all thirteen years and eleven months of it, and I can assure you that you won't be bored because my life has been very different from that of anyone else I know. It's not that I've sailed the seven seas or anything exotic like that, but . . . well, you'd better read on and find out.

I was born on May 6th 1971, the daughter of Carol and Anthony Woollard, and christened Margaret Joanna. I spent the first six years of my life in Rugby, a small town in the Midlands, and was very happy there. I was given a lot of love and affection, coming from a close-knit family and being the only child up until the age of three, when my sister Eleanor was born.

I've always been close to my sister. She's more like a friend really and we talk about a lot of things, most of them pure nonsense! I remember her birth quite clearly – going on a long bus journey with my dad to see her in hospital and being jealous when she came home and stole all the attention. When we were little we used to knock on each other's bedroom walls and we had a special knocking code.

In Rugby there was a cemetery a few doors away from our house and I used to ride around it on my little red tricycle. The first things I ever read were the names on the gravestones. There were two parks nearby and I used to call them the Little Park and the Big Park. We had a big garden and I used to like having my tea under the apple tree which I called 'Noddy's house'.

The best times we've had as a family, indeed some of my happiest memories, have been on holiday. One that really sticks out in my mind is in Eastbourne when I was five. There was a drought that summer and we were only allowed to have baths once a week. I remember there was a station on the local train line called Polgate and I thought it would be funny if I used Colgate toothpaste at Polgate, so I brushed my teeth on the train and left the toothbrush behind!

Margaret

My earliest days 1

When I was two, I went into the jungle (a little wood) with my dad. I wore jeans and a jumper just like my dad and had a rucksack the same as my dad's. When we went into the jungle we collected leaves, about a dozen at a time, then I'd go home and tell my mum which leaf was the lion or the tiger or the elephant from the jungle. Also when my mum was pregnant with my sister I used to run away from her because I knew she couldn't catch me, and sometimes when we went into the market, I used to get lost on purpose and walk around the sweet stall and start to cry just so as I could stand on the bench and eat sweets.

Beth

I was born in East Africa in a small town by the name of Kakuru. I stayed there, at my 'Mamsi's' (mother's brother), for just over six months. We then moved to Mombasa. Here we lived in a large apartment with my 'Kakaji' (father's brother). We had a household help by the name of Ali.

I remember that when I was around three years old, I was asleep in my parents' bed. My father was at work, my mother was out shopping and Ali was busy with the housework. Avani, my sister, who is younger than me, was asleep in her cot. I woke up feeling very thirsty. I looked around the bed for my bottle but to my dismay could not find it. I noticed a bottle on the floor with transparent liquid inside it. I jumped out of the large bed and walked towards the bottle. I drank it and later felt a burning pain inside my stomach. That moment my mother walked in and I passed out. In later life I was told that the paraffin had been pumped out of my stomach by means of tubes and I was lucky to be alive.

Sabir

My earliest days 1

In pairs or groups, discuss these questions:

- Look at the way each writer has started his or her account. How has each writer tried to catch the reader's attention? Which beginning do you prefer and why?
- Which of the extracts do you think were from memories – and which were stories told to the writers by other people? What clues can you find to help you decide?
- How far back can *you* remember? Talk about your earliest memory, and any stories other people have told you about your early life.

Now you can begin to plan your own autobiographical account.

Research In class, make a rough list of things you can remember from your earliest days. It doesn't need to be a whole story. It might be impressions of things, feelings, people's faces, smells, food, places, colours or animals. At home, ask two or three people who knew you well before you were five to tell you stories about yourself. Write them down in rough before you forget them. Ask if you can look at your birth certificate and photos that might trigger new stories and memories.

Drafting Look at your rough notes and decide what order you're going to put the stories in. Think about your opening sentence: you need to make your reader immediately interested.
Here are some opening sentences used by writers like you:

'Here I am, sitting in my play pen, bored stiff. I don't want to play with my aeroplane, nor with my big ted, so I decide to go for a walk.'

'There my mum was, sat on the settee, talking to my dad about me when she had to be rushed to hospital to have – ME!

'It happened on the eleventh of August 1977, the most important thing in history, I, Richard, was born.'

Choose how you are going to start, then write your *first draft*.

TASK 2 My earliest days 2

Aim To revise and redraft your autobiographical account of 'My earliest days'

Here is a first draft by a student called Waseem:

My earliest days

When I was four years old I was in nursery biting a boy because I wanted to play with the toys. At the age of three I went to the zoo. I was looking around when I put my finger in a cage and a bird bit me. It wasn't too serious, though after that I never wanted to go to the zoo again. When I was two years old I was in Pakistan trying to shake a tree to get some plums off when suddenly a plum hit me on the head and another landed on the ground by me. I ate both of them, then went home and was sick all over the floor.

- Working with a partner, improve Waseem's first draft. Look at the order he's given to early events in his life; how would you advise him to improve it? Look at the way he's started his story: can you suggest a better opening sentence?

- On your own, write an improved second draft of Waseem's account. Then compare what you've written with your partner.

- Finally, as his story will still be short and there must be many other things he could tell you about his early life, write down four or five questions you would ask to prompt him to tell you more about the events he's included.

- Show your partner your first draft and discuss together how you might redraft it.

TASK
3

A day like any other

Aim To tell a reader what your life is like by focusing on four typical moments and describing a day in your life

One of the best ways of helping people to know you is by inviting them to share a typical day in your life.

The happy family at breakfast time, relaxing over a bowl of Weeties. You'd never know this was Saturday!

Me and Claire, busy...

Me and my best mate, Andrew, spending a HUGE sum of money on nothing.

Peace and quiet, on my own at last.

A day like any other

Working in pairs, each choose a non-school day, either at the weekend or during the holiday.

- List four moments from the day.
- Imagine that someone has caught each moment in a photograph: write down everything which will appear in the four pictures.
- Using the present tense, draft four accounts of what you are doing at each moment. Explain what is happening, describe the scene, make the reader see and hear everything with you, and report what you're thinking and saying.

Think about your *audience*: a reader who does not know you should be able to get a picture of what a day in your life is like.

- Show your draft to your partner and discuss whether you have left out any important details.
- Redraft your account, adding any details your partner suggested.

Family scenes

Aim To write and record a short radio script of a typical everyday family scene

One way of telling the story of your life is in the form of a playscript, so that actors can bring your written words to life on stage or in the studio. On Sheet 8 is the start of a family story written as a play.

- In groups, practise reading this script and then make a tape-recording of it. You could find an appropriate piece of music or some sound effects to set the scene.

  What do you think is going to happen next? Discuss the different ways that the plot of this play could develop.

  Write the next scene for this play. As you do, think about how each of the four characters behave in the opening scene. Make sure that how they behave in your scene fits in with the impression you get of them in the opening scene. Remember that it is a radio play and that any actions and movements people make have to be explained by what is *said* rather than by stage directions.

  Make a tape-recording of your script. Listen to each other's scripts and talk about what works well and how you could improve them.

- Role play a typical family scene. Either decide on a situation of your own or role play one of these situations:

  an incident on a family picnic

  an early morning scene when everyone is rushing to get to work/school.

  an incident at a family event e.g. a birthday party, a wedding, a christening.

- Write a short script for a radio play based on a family situation. Include at least three characters. Before you begin, decide what impression you want to give the audience of each of the characters. Try to hear how each character sounds as you write the words s/he speaks.

  When you have finished your first draft, ask three or four friends to join you in a trial read-through. Be critical and be prepared to change words or speeches.

  Form groups of four and tape-record your scripts.

Family scenes

Lay by

FATHER, BEN, TRICIA, MOTHER. *Father under the car.*

FATHER: Pass me that. . .
BEN: What?
FATHER: Spanner.
BEN: What spanner?
FATHER: The spanner. Don't you know what a spanner is? Don't they teach you anything at your school?
BEN: No.
MOTHER: Is it going to be fixed?
FATHER: I'm trying.
MOTHER: No need to get irritable, just tell me.
FATHER: I can't tell you. Just be patient.
MOTHER: We'll never get to Alton Towers at this rate.
TRICIA: Angela's been there before. She told me. She's been twice. Went on all the rides. They have the biggest rides in Europe. When you go down them you think you're going to die. Angela said.
BEN: Oh shut up about Angela.
MOTHER: Don't talk like that Ben. Angela's a very attractive girl.
BEN: Yeah to the other vampires.
MOTHER: That's not funny. Now stop it.
TRICIA: Angela says Daddy works for her father's firm. Does that mean he's Daddy's boss?
MOTHER: That'll do Tricia.
TRICIA: Does it?
FATHER: Yes he is, and if Mr High and Mighty Travers sees me under this car I'll never hear the last of it.
BEN: I've seen his car. Better than this wreck.
FATHER: Ben!
TRICIA: Angela says they have a new car every year.
MOTHER: Oh shut up about Angela for goodness sake.

Gareth Owen

ASSIGNMENT 2 DESCRIBING PEOPLE

TASK 1

Pen portraits

Aim To write brief pen portraits which capture the character of people you know well

- Work with a friend:

  Read 'A bit of advice' on Sheet 10. Draw two columns. Label one column *Appearance* and the other column *Behaviour*. In each column write down what you learn from Jonathan's descriptions about the appearance and behaviour of a) Jenny, b) Daniel, c) Jonathan himself.

  In one or two sentences, try to sum up the advice Uncle Leopold gives Jonathan.

- Prepare to write a collection of three or four pen portraits of people you know well. Begin by making notes about each of them. Think about

  what she or he looks like

  what she or he does that makes you laugh, annoys you or that you like

  things that seem to sum each person up: likes and dislikes; hobbies; sayings; habits.

  stories about them.

  Show each other your notes and help each other in the way that Uncle Leopold helped Jonathan. Get your partner to tell you what the person is really like by asking questions about how she or he behaves. Suggest obviously exaggerated descriptions that your partner will want to correct.

- When you have finished discussing each of the people, write your pen portraits. Before you write each portrait, decide exactly what impression you want to give of that person and select the details from your notes that will help you to give that impression. Keep your descriptions short, like this description of someone's father:

> **My father**
> My father is a big man with wild black hair. When he laughs, the sun laughs in the window-panes. When he thinks, you can almost see his thoughts sitting on all the tables and chairs. When he is angry, me and my brother Huey shiver to the bottom of our shoes.

Pen portraits

A bit of advice

Jonathan wants to write a book about his family and the adventures they have had together. His Uncle Leopold offers him some good advice.

Uncle Leopold was standing in front of the fire, warming his behind. He had just read that bit I wrote. He was sucking at his pipe, making it splutter and gurgle.

'Is it any good?' I asked.

'Splendid. Keep the sentences short. You'd better shove in a description of you all. Otherwise anyone who reads it won't know what you look like.'

'I'm not keen on descriptions,' I said. 'They're boring. When I read a book, I usually skip the descriptions and turn over the pages until the next thing happens.'

'Oh do you?' Uncle Leopold said. 'I don't mean anything elaborate. You know the kind of thing. Something like "my sister is short and fat and covered with black hairy warts".'

'She's not. That's horrible. She's nothing like that at all.'

'It's only an example.'

'But you know Jenny's not like that. She's thin and all healthy brown-coloured, with freckles on her face and those big gaps between her front teeth, and straight brown hair and a fringe. And she's usually quite friendly.'

'There you are then,' Uncle Leopold said. 'In a nutshell. Shove it in. Write it down. But keep the sentences short. How would you describe Daniel?'

Daniel! I thought for a minute. It's a peculiar thing about describing people. Inside your head, you know exactly what they are like, but when it comes to writing it down it's not so easy. In the end, I said:

'I don't think I can possibly describe Daniel.'

'Rubbish,' Uncle Leopold laughed. 'It's simple. He's a jolly, good-tempered, matey chap, short and fat and . . .'

'No he's not,' I shouted. 'You know he isn't. He pretends to be grown up, although he isn't yet, and he's sarcastic and tries to make out he's bored with everything. He's quite tall, and not

▶ *Pen portraits*

A bit of advice

at all fat. His voice is breaking and that makes him angrier, because he thinks it sounds funny. He's got a bony sort of face, and blue eyes, and his hair is lighter than Jenny's, but wavy.'

Taking his pipe from his mouth, Uncle Leo said:

'That seems a first-rate description to me. Better write it down before you forget it. Now how would you describe yourself, Jonathan?'

'I'm not going to put anything like that in,' I said. 'No fear.'

'Of course you must. Come on.'

I didn't say anything.

'Come on, Jonathan,' Uncle Leopold insisted.

'To begin with, I'm a bit weedy.'

'Nonsense. You're not weedy at all.'

'And everyone keeps saying that I'm anxious and nervous. I have to wear these glasses because I'm short-sighted. I wish they wouldn't keep slipping down my nose. The trouble is they don't fit properly. Or perhaps my nose slopes down too much.'

'It's a perfectly good nose,' Uncle Leopold said indignantly. 'It's the same shape as mine. You're very fortunate to take after me instead of your father.'

'Then perhaps it's because the frame is bent. And I think I'm different from Jenny and Daniel. For one thing, I've got brown eyes and dark hair, and I'm much quieter. I don't talk as much as Daniel, or rush about like Jenny.'

'That'll do fine.'

from The Frog Report *by Benjamin Lee*

YR 7

(photos to
stimulate)
narrative /
thought

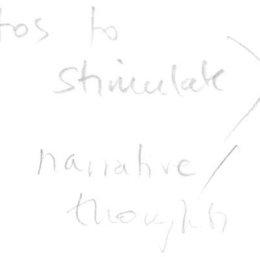

TASK 2 *Snapshot poems*

Aim To write snapshot poems describing people in action based on close observation of them doing something

Instead of a photo album, there is a collection of snapshot poems on Sheet 13.

- Working in pairs, each choose one of the snapshot poems. Try to picture what you would see if the action described in the poem had been captured in a photograph. Make a list of the words and phrases which helped you to build up that picture. Then, take it in turns to describe to each other exactly what is happening in the poem and which words and phrases helped you to form a picture of the person in your mind.

- On your own, choose a person you can see from your place in the room. Observe closely what she or he is doing: e.g. resting an elbow on the table, hand on chin, lost in thought; clutching a pencil, scribbling furiously; leaning over a book, flicking through the pages. Or observe what the teacher is doing, or someone you can see through the window – a painter or a gardener.

  Decide what impression you want the reader to get from your 'snapshot' poem. For example, you might want to show how carefully the gardener is planting bulbs. When you start to write, choose the details that will help you to put across the impression you want to create.

- When you have done a first draft, swap your 'snapshot' poems for your partner to comment on.

- On your own, write three or four snapshots. You can write in prose, or choose poems. You can find subjects anywhere, either live – people you see on the bus, shopping, in the park, on a building site – or in action photographs.

  Remember:

  observe first

  jot down details

  decide what impression you want to create

  select details and give it a shape by putting a detail on each line

  keep it short.

▶ *Snapshot poems*

The Artist

Mr T.
>   bareheaded
>   in a soiled undershirt
his hair standing out
>   on all sides
>   stood on his toes
heels together
>   arms gracefully
>   for the moment
curled above his head.
>   Then he whirled about
>   bounded
into the air
>   and with an entrechat
>   perfectly achieved
completed the figure.
>   My mother
>   taken by surprise
where she sat
>   in her invalid's chair
>   was left speechless.
Bravo! she cried at last
>   and clapped her hands.
>   The man's wife
came from the kitchen:
>   What goes on here? she said.
>   But the show was over.
>   *William Carlos Williams*

Mother shelling peas

The sun shone strongly through the window
Lighting up the dancing particles of dust
Making mother's hair gleam
Like polished brass
Shining on her black shoes
On the red tiles
As she perched on the kitchen stool
Shelling peas.
Mother's hands are quick and deft
As they move from pod to pod
Throwing empty pods in one pile
And picking up a fresh one
From the brown paper bag
Like a fisherman, gutting fish.

> *Katherine Board*

The penknife glides

The penknife glides through the polystyrene,
turning it to get a good angle.
Smoothly the oiled blade cuts
as my dad carves a goldfish.
All his face is screwed up.
He sees nothing but his moving hand,
and doesn't know I'm there.
Hands last night that were rough, big and clumsy
as the floorboards were torn up,
and thick cable cut to lay beneath.
Now, as I watch,
I wonder at the care of his delicate hands,
As a small perfect goldfish forms.

> *Ian Griffiths*

T A S K
3 *A detailed description*

YR 7

Aim To write a detailed description of a person – her appearance, character and habits

On Sheets 15 and 16 a young writer describes her grandmother. As you read it, notice how your impression of Gran is built up as a result of the details describing what she does and what she says.

- Re-read Valerie Avery's description of her Gran and make notes on what you learn about a) Gran's appearance, b) Gran's habits, c) Gran's character. Write down why you think Valerie liked her Gran and decide whether or not you think you would have liked Gran. Then, form groups and compare what you have written.

  Discuss how Valerie has structured her description of her Gran. How is it divided into sections? Decide what the topic of each of the main sections is and draw a flow-chart or diagram showing how Valerie has shaped her description of her Gran.

- Using the information Valerie gives you in her detailed description, write a brief pen portrait of Gran in which you try to give the same impression of her as Valerie does. Keep your descriptions brief – a maximum of 80 words.

- Decide on a person you know well and prepare to write a portrait. Like Valerie you will need to make your reader:
  1 picture the person by describing her/his appearance, movements, where s/he lives/works
  2 hear the person's voice by including snatches of conversation and stories s/he tells
  3 get to know the person by describing some of her/his habits
  4 share your thoughts and feelings about her/him.

  Start by jotting down details about your subject in any order, as they come to you. Then, before beginning to draft your portrait, decide how to give it a shape. Look again at Valerie's description of her Gran. Notice how she begins by describing what Gran is usually doing when she arrives to visit her, then reveals her character through the conversations and habits she describes. Decide what would be the best way to start your description.

▶ *A detailed description*

Gran

I liked Gran; she was so different from Mum. Because Mum left for work early in the morning I would go downstairs and talk to Gran while waiting to go to school. She sat in her armchair before the fire, wearing an old red dressing-gown, cooking her breakfast; she toasted bread on a fork, or held a rasher of bacon before the flames with one hand catching the drips of fat on a slice of bread which she held in her other hand. When it was cooked she put it on a plate which had already been used twice that morning: first for Steve's breakfast of bacon and mushrooms and then, when he left for work, grandad cleaned the plate with a slice of bread while waiting for his bacon and eggs to be dished up. The over-worked plate was smeared with yolk and bits of bacon curled round the edge. While Gran ate I did all the talking. I told her about school.

'We're learning French now, Gran. Quelle heure est-il? D'you know what that means?'

'Gawd knows.'

'It means: What's the time?'

'Oh does it. Can't see the point meself. Steve says they all talk English in every country, and 'e's seen almost every country on 'is bike, so what's the point? But tell me some more about that science teacher of yours.'

I envied Gran sitting in her chair with the dog at her feet, toasting her breakfast in her warm, sleepy kitchen. I wished I could be her and not have to go to school, while she kept wishing she were my age. Her motto was 'Here today, gone tomorrow.' Mum said it was bad for me to listen to her morbid talk, but I was fascinated by tales of hospitals, funerals, and deaths.

'This woman 'ad no inside. She 'ad to live on boiled eggs and water, and 'er 'usband 'e 'ad no arms, blown off in the war they was, so 'e 'ad to manage with two 'ooks. Turned you up to look at 'im, but the funny thing is they both lived to a ripe old age, whereas 'is brother was a big 'ealthy bloke, strong as 'orse 'e was, never 'ad a day's illness in 'is life. One day 'e 'ad 'is dinner, big eater 'e was, 'e 'ad steak and kidney pud, that was his favourite grub, an' 'e says to his wife: "I think I'll take the dog for a walk in the park." So 'e goes out. But 'e never came back. Dropped down dead outside the baker's 'e did. Just like that.'

While she talked to me, she washed her face and hands in a large mixing bowl which she stood on the kitchen table and

● 15

▶ *A detailed description*

Gran

was filled to the brim with boiling water. The red, strong-smelling soap rested on a saucer while she covered her face with a creamy pink lather, then sluiced it off, cupping her hands several times with water and sounding, as she put her face into it, as though she were drinking a bowl of soup. With water dripping from her chins and her eyes stinging with soap, she groped around blindly for the towel, tugging first at the tablecloth, then at the curtains, until she realised that it was still hanging on the line over the range.

'Give us the towel, there's a good girl,' she'd say. 'Quick now. It doesn't matter if you can't find it, anything 'll do, so long as it's not yer Grandad's combinations.'

It took her about half an hour to dress herself because she wore so many layers of clothes; petticoat upon petticoat, all of different colours and different lengths, waited in a queue to move up nearer to her skin each morning, and each was fastened by dozens of hooks and buttons.

'Yer need plenty of clothes when yer gets to my age, because yer feel the cold somethin' terrible yer do. Goes straight to yer bones it does and gives yer rheumaticks if yer don't wrap proper.'

Finally she combed her grey, greasy hair that was usually lank, but if she was going to a special jumble sale that day, or to her old age pensioners' club, she forced it to curl by using her iron curling tongs. She would sit in her arm-chair and wait for the tortuous tongs to turn red-hot in the fire then, catching a strand of hair in a scorching grasp, she twisted the tongs round and round until they could go no further. For a few seconds they were held taut while she waited for the miracle to happen.

'Does it hurt, Gran?'

'Not 'alf,' she said. 'Burnin' me brains out, it is, but it's worth it. The 'otter the tongs the longer me curls stay in.'

'Won't your hair catch alight?'

'It will if I keep 'em in too long. There, I think I'm done now,' and she pulled out the tongs leaving behind a long grey, sizzling sausage.

from London Morning *by Valerie Avery*

16 •

T A S K
4

A life story through interview

Aim To interview a person and use what is said as the basis for writing part of her/his life story

Read Barbara's interview with her grandmother about life during the Second World War (Sheet 17).

Decide on an older person you know well who wouldn't mind helping you. Ask her/him if you can conduct an interview to find out about a time in her/his life. You could, like Barbara, find out about life during the Second World War; or about childhood earlier this century; or about being the same age as you several years ago; or about being at work.

- Write five or six 'starter' questions for your interview. You might add to them later if your interview goes well. Make sure your questions can't just be answered 'yes' or 'no'.

- Interview your subject. If you can, tape it; otherwise, write notes as your subject talks.

- Decide how you're going to present what you've discovered from your subject. This could be:

  either a transcript of the interview (like Barbara's) recording your subject's own words. Introduce the interview with a brief portrait of the person.

  or a chapter from your subject's life story or *biography*. Use what you've discovered from the interview to write his/her life story in your own words. Here's how part of Barbara's biography of her grandmother might begin:

> While Grandma was living out in the country Hull was badly bombed. They hardly heard the noise the bombs made, but Grandma was horrified to see what they'd done to the city when she went to visit her father in hospital.

A life story through interview

These are extracts from Barbara's interview with her grandma about life during the Second World War.

Have you any special or sad memories from the War?
Yes, I remember once when Hull had been bombed severely. We were living out in Riplingham then and we weren't bombed and barely heard what was going on in Hull. At this time my father was in hospital so I had biked ten miles into Hull to go and see him. When I got there I just stood horrified. All I could see was rubble, fire engines and smoke. There were hardly any buildings left standing, only half the hospital was left. I was worried about my father's safety, but luckily he was fine.

Can you remember about the barrage balloons?
Yes, I remember one night looking out of my window to find that the barrage balloons looked to be rising. This probably meant we were going to have a raid. I couldn't sleep and about an hour later I went to the window and opened the curtains to see that the sky was almost on fire, it was that bright with bombers and fires everywhere.

What was the closest you came to death?
Well actually it was whilst I was at home. We owned a shop and my father had just closed up when the air raid siren rang out. My father heard the aeroplanes coming so he called us all to hurry up and go to the shelter next door. My sister wouldn't go and said we must wait until the bombs from the plane had landed. If we had gone then we would not be here now, as it had destroyed nearly all of the street and the pavement outside where we would have been walking.

TASK 1

My neighbourhood

YR 7 ?

Aim To write short descriptions which capture the atmosphere of a number of places you know well

No two houses, streets, villages or towns are exactly the same. Every place has its own particular look or atmosphere. This is from a story by Michael Anthony in which he describes his walk to school in Port of Spain, Trinidad.

Enchanted alley

Leaving for school early in the mornings, I walked slowly through the busy parts of the town. The business places would all be opening then and smells of strange fragrance would fill the High Street. Inside the opening doors I would see clerks dusting, arranging, hanging things up, getting ready for the day's business. They looked cheerful and eager and they opened the doors very wide. Sometimes I stood up to watch them.

In places between the stores several little alleys ran off the High Street. Some were busy and some were not, and there was one that was long and narrow and dark and very strange. Here too the shops would be opening as I passed, and there would be bearded men spreading rugs on the pavement. There would be women also, with veils thrown over their shoulders, setting up their stalls and chatting in a strange sweet tongue. Often I stood, too, watching them, and taking in the fragrance of rugs and spices and onions and sweetmeats. And sometimes, suddenly remembering, I would hurry away for fear the school-bell had gone.

In class, long after I settled down, the thoughts of this alley would return to me. I would recall certain stalls and certain beards and certain flashing eyes, and even some of the rugs that had been rolled out. The women, too, with bracelets around their ankles and around their sun-browned arms flashed to my mind. I could almost picture them laughing together and talking in that strange, sweet tongue. And mostly the day would be quite old before the spell of the alley wore off in my mind.

My neighbourhood

In pairs, look back at the description on Sheet 19 to discover *why* this street and alley cast a 'spell' on Michael. Now, make three lists of what he could see, hear and smell.

Use some of the ideas you have learned from this to start planning short descriptions of places you know.

- Make two columns headed like this:

  The area near my home   *The centre of my village/town*

  Together write down under each heading as many places with special character as you can.

- Choose three or four places from each of the columns and begin writing by yourself. Picture each place in your head before you write – or, better still, visit it and make notes. Your aim is to help your listener or reader to experience the atmosphere; to see, hear and smell each place with you.

- Read and comment on each other's work in draft form before you finish. Decide what order your pieces will be read or presented in. You could start from home and move outwards, or you could finish back at home. Write an introduction together telling people some general things about where you live.

- Practise reading, then tape-record your descriptions.
  or make attractive copies of your pieces for a display.

DRAFTING

Thomas included under column 1 – the empty house; the river foreshore; where we used to have a den; the chip shop. Under column 2 he included – the ice rink; Queen's Gardens; the Transport Museum and the Docks.

Before you start, discuss with your partner how well you think Thomas has helped you to imagine visiting the Docks in this description.

The docks are not all that far away from my home and I just cross Walker's Farm and mind that he does not shoot rock salt at me because he will try to hurt you if he can. I always cross with great care. Ringed plovers nest near the farm each year. From the Docks you can see the trawlers coming down the river from the Antarctic fishing grounds. My father is a skipper on the freezer trawlers and he goes away from home for twelve weeks at a time. When he returns he docks in the new dock and he will smell the freshness of the land and of the sea.

YR 7

TASK 2 *A perfect place to live*

Aim To design your ideal home and to put together a factual description of it, using drawings and plans

In small groups, study the drawings on Sheet 22. If you had enough money and could choose, which of these buildings would you choose to live in?

- Imagine what the building might be like inside. Choose one room – a bedroom, living room, games room or studio. Tell each other exactly how you would furnish or decorate it.

- On your own, write a letter to an interior designer explaining how you want the room to be designed. Include rough drawings or diagrams if this helps to communicate what you want.

- Imagine that you could have a house designed and built exactly to your plans for you (and your family, if you wish) to live in. Think about all the things which are important to you:

  Where would it be?

  What shape would the house be?

  What range of rooms would you have?

  Are there any special features you would like?

- Draw up your brief for the architect (and interior designer, if you wish).

  1 Make plans and drawings – these can be kept simple for the architect to work from, but need to convey clearly what you want.

  2 Include notes to accompany your plans and drawings. These might be on

     the situation of the house

     the different rooms you want

     any special features

  In your notes, explain why these things are important to you.

  You may need to draft and re-draft your drawings and notes before you feel ready to make a display of your work.

If you've ever fantasised about living in a treehouse in a tropical country, or at the top of a castle in the highlands, now is your chance to enact your fantasy!

A perfect place to live

YR 8

© Judith Atkinson and John Foster, 1991. Talking and Writing from Experience, Macmillan English. Copyright restrictions on p. ii.

TASK
3

A place I'll always remember

Aim To plan, draft and write a detailed description of a place telling readers why you remember it clearly

In the extract on Sheet 24 Dirk Bogarde describes the gully near their home where he and his sister often played and where she took him one day to show him a surprise.

- In groups, study these statements about the gully. Which of them do you think most accurately describes the gully?

  A A bleak, rather forbidding place

  B A shady, secluded place

  C A wild overgrown place teeming with wildlife

  D A dank, decaying place full of rubbish

- What impression of the gully do you think Dirk Bogarde wants to give the reader? Pick out all the details that he includes which help him to convey that impression.

- Imagine you work for a publisher who wants to produce an illustration of the gully. Write the brief (the set of instructions) telling the artist which details of the gully you want her to include in her drawing and what impression of the gully you want her picture to give. (Note: You could include a rough sketch of the gully to give an idea of what you require.)

- On your own, plan, draft and write a detailed description of a place you remember well for some reason. It could be a place where you and your friends used to play, somewhere you visited on an outing or holiday, or somewhere that you remember clearly because of an incident that occurred there.

  First, try to picture the place clearly in your mind and jot down as many details of it as you can. Then, think about what impression of the place you want to give your readers. Underline all those details which would help you to create that impression and, as you develop your writing, try to work them into your description.

  When you have completed your first draft, show it to a friend. Ask him/her to read it and to tell you what impression s/he gets of the place from your description of it. Does s/he get a clear enough picture of the place or do you need to add any further details?

23

► *A place I'll always remember*

The gully

'Come on,' she said, taking my arm, 'let's go down to the gully. I've got something marvellous to show you. You will be surprised. Come on.' And because I hadn't anything else to do at that moment I went with her. We clambered up the hill outside the fence, to the top, and reached the big wood where the gully was hidden. It was cool and green and damp smelling under the trees; the sides of the gully were all big lumps of chalk with funny roots tangling about and long trails of ivy and deadly nightshade. It was very quiet in there; you could just hear the wind moving about in the tops of the trees and the noise of our feet slithering in the muddy ruts of the floor.

There were voles down there, and hedgehogs too. We used to hear them at dusk squeaking and rustling about in the leaves looking for slugs. Which we thought rather disgusting. And once we found a great toad with golden eyes bulging in a little cave place in the chalk. It was almost as big as a plate and when we carried it back to the house and showed Lally she covered her face with her hands and threw the darning at us. 'Take the horrible thing away!' she cried. 'It'll give you warts you'll see. Take it out this instant.' She was really awfully silly about toads. She didn't mind anything else almost, except cows, but she was scared out of her wits by a humble, nice looking old toad.

But there weren't any toads down in the gully this morning. And we twisted along through the old cart ruts and brambles until my sister told me to stop, and there in front of me was a great pile of old tin cans and bits of bedsteads and rusty wire. It was just an old rubbish dump. Nothing exciting at all.

'I can't possibly be surprised by an old rubbish dump,' I said. 'And anyway, I've seen it before. It's been here for years and years.'

My sister was rooting about in the tins and bits of old iron bedsteads, there were tangles of old chicken wire and an oil stove with a broken door lying in a clutter of pram wheels and shards of a broken plough.

Suddenly, amidst all the clanking and clonking my sister gave a cry and called out: 'Shut your eyes. This is the surprise!'

from A Postillion Struck by Lightning *by Dirk Bogarde*

TASK 1

My interests 1

English

YR 6/7/8

Aim To present a talk on a subject that interests you

- On your own, prepare a talk to give to a group of four or five people in the class about a hobby in which you are interested. Collect your ideas by doing a brainstorm and then grouping your ideas under headings.

- Show your list of headings to a partner and discuss the best order in which to present them in your talk.

- Try to think of a dramatic way to start your talk, which will capture the attention of the rest of the group, and of a way of ending the talk, so that it does not end too abruptly or on a low note.

- Make a set of cards with headings and notes on them to refer to during your talk. Then, form groups and give your talks.

- After each talk, tell the person who gave it what you thought were the strengths and weaknesses of the talk. Discuss

    the content What was the most interesting part? What further information would have made it more interesting?

    the structure Was there a good beginning and a good ending? Were the points in the best possible order?

    the delivery What was good about the delivery? How could it be improved? (Think about pace, volume, tone.) Finally, decide whose talk was most effective and why.

TASK 2 *My interests 2*   YRS 7 + 8

Aim To write a short article for people of your own age about a hobby or sport that interests you, explaining how you first became interested in it and why you enjoy it

- In pairs, read Joelle's account on Sheet 27 of how she started water-skiing.
- Study the first paragraph. How does she try to capture the reader's attention? Do you think she succeeds in doing so?
- How else could she have started? Draft an alternative opening paragraph, then compare your paragraph with those which other pairs have drafted. Which is the most effective – one of yours or the opening Joelle used?
- Discuss how Joelle keeps the reader's attention

  by letting the reader know her thoughts and feelings

  by putting in interesting information about water-skiing.

  Underline or highlight examples of places where she does this.
- Talk about the final paragraph. Do you think it is an effective ending? Suggest an alternative way that she could have ended the article.

On your own, draft an article for people of your own age about a hobby or sport that interests you. (You could use the notes you made for your talk as the basis of your article.)

Think of an interesting way of starting and try to let your reader know your thoughts and feelings about the subject in the way that Joelle lets us know how she feels about water-skiing.

My interests 2
Water-skiing

Four years ago, I was offered the chance to go water-skiing by my mum's boyfriend Chris. I remember thinking on the journey up to the lake in South Cerney, Gloucestershire, I wonder if anybody will mind if I don't try the ski-jump today. The fact is — I didn't even get up on the skis that day!

As I stood at the lakeside, I was terrified with excitement and soon I was freezing cold. I had borrowed Chris's sister's wetsuit. It was a bit too big for me and I remember the horrible experience of the water slowly seeping through to my skin — first round my ankles, then round my knees and finally all the way up to my neck. I was soaking wet and cold and the boat hadn't even started moving.

The idea was that I would first go round the lake lying flat on a board, which had a sponge mat on it to stop you from slipping. I squeaked 'Hit it!' the term you use when you are ready to go. You don't say 'Go!' as it could be confused with 'No!'

I'd been given lots of instructions what to do, but by the time I was in the water, lying on the board, I had forgotten most of them. The boat engine revved and . . . I felt the board nose-dive to some unknown depth — for some unknown reason.

The boat returned and circled me a few times, while Chris told me to make sure that the front of the board was *above* the surface of the water when the boat accelerated. Then, we tried again.

That was my first taste of water-skiing, even if I wasn't on skis. It wasn't long before I progressed to kneeling on the board, although the technique of getting from a lying position to kneeling up, whilst being pulled around a Gloucestershire reservoir at fifteen miles an hour, must have appeared rather odd to any onlookers.

When I tried the skis on for the first time, I felt as if I was being turned upside down. Then, when eventually they were on and the boat moved away, the tow rope wound around me. I grabbed it and was pulled in a complete circle. I lost my balance again, so the boat returned. Chris put me the right way round and up and we tried again — and again and again.

I can now get out of the water almost every time and stay up for two laps of the lake without stopping. I've learned when starting to remember to keep the ski tips together and to stay in a crouched position and to let the boat pull you up.

After four years and a total of about ten visits to the lake, I can now water-ski. It's a really exhilarating experience. But like everything else, it takes lots of practice. It will be a long time before I can try to do any of the difficult things you see the experts doing on TV!

Joelle

TASK 3 Customs and celebrations

Yrs 6/7/8

Aim To write an article explaining the customs and celebrations that are part of your life to someone who lives in another country

- In pairs, study Nazea's article about Ramadan and Eid (Sheet 29). What different types of information about Ramadan does it contain? Think up a heading for each type of information, then draw a flow-chart showing how the article is organised.

- Study Lina's article about Diwali (Sheet 30). Talk about the information it contains and draw a flow-chart showing how it is organised. Then, compare the two flow-charts.

- Compare the style of Nazea's article with the style of Lina's article. Which would you say is the more personal style? Which article do you think was written for someone in particular and which was written for a more general audience? Explain why.

- On your own, write an article about a custom or celebration that is part of your life. Before you begin, make a list of headings describing the types of information you are going to include and decide what order you are going to put them in. Decide whether you are writing for a general audience or for someone in particular and use an appropriate style.

Customs and celebrations

Ramadan and Eid

Once a year all Muslims above the age of ten fast for a month. In the Islamic calendar this is the ninth month, which is summer time. This makes it a greater burden to fast, with the humid weather.

The month of Ramadan started when the Quran, or holy book, was revealed by the angel Gabriel to the Prophet Muhammed. The period of fasting lasts from dawn until sunset every day.

One should not allow food or drink to pass one's lips. Smoking is not allowed either. After sunset the fast is broken by some light refreshment and the traditional breakfast takes place just before dawn.

During Ramadan Muslims should avoid thoughts, words or anything that would ruin the fast, as one must stay clean, use sweet language and be respectful. If these points are ignored then the fast is broken.

Some people are excused the fast – those who are sick, pregnant women and people who have very heavy work to do. However, they are expected to make up for it later.

There are several reasons for fasting. One is to make a Muslim aware of the reality of hunger in the world. Another reason is that the fasting gives self-discipline, when the mind rules over the physical demands of the body. A change of lifestyle can be directed to Allah to show self-awareness: this gives one the opportunity to live the true Islamic lifestyle.

The last ten days of the fast are more like celebrations. These are known as 'the holy night of power and revelation' when the Angel and the Spirit descend by the leave of the Lord.

At the end of the fast, the feast of Eid-ul-fitr, the second of the great Muslim feasts, takes place. It lasts for four days. Friends and relatives get together in the celebrations. It marks the end of the hardships of Ramadan.

Nazea

Customs and celebrations

Diwali

We've been having a good time because we've been celebrating Diwali, which is the Hindu festival of lights. According to tradition, on this day thousands of years ago, Lord Rama with his beautiful Queen Sita, and loving brother Lakshama, returned to his kingdom after 14 years of exile. The people of Ayoda were so overjoyed to see Rama that they lit the city with lamps and danced in the streets.

Everyone gets so excited at Diwali, just as people do at Christmas. But the first part of the day is rather boring. You have to get up early, have a bath, then go to the temple to pray.

Afterwards, there is a family gathering. We went to our cousins' house. They had decorated the house in the traditional way by drawing some rangali on the floor. These are patterns and pictures of gods, flowers and animals. We talked and danced round the pictures, while the little children played games and told jokes. Next we had the food, which includes sweets and Indian sweets, which are really nice.

When it started to get dark, we lit up the windows with candles and there was more dancing. Then, when it was really dark, we went outside and the day ended with a firework display. Fortunately, it wasn't raining and we had a great time.

The day after Diwali is our New Year's Day. That's when we give each other presents. My parents gave me some new clothes and a beautiful new brush and comb set.

Lina

TASK
1

First person narrative

Aim To write about a personal experience, telling readers your thoughts and feelings as well as describing what happened

- In groups, read Neil McIntosh's account of his escapade (Sheet 32). As you read it, what were you thinking about? Did it remind you of any escapades or narrow escapes that you have had? Write down what you were thinking, then share your thoughts and memories in a group discussion.

- As well as telling us what happened, Neil McIntosh lets the reader know what his thoughts and feelings were throughout the experience. On a piece of paper, draw two columns. Label one column *The events* and the other *Thoughts and feelings*. Go through the story carefully, listing the events that happen and what Neil McIntosh's thoughts and feelings were at each point.

- On your own, choose a personal experience that you remember clearly, and write about it as Neil McIntosh does, describing what happened. Capture your thoughts and feelings for your reader to share.

© Judith Atkinson and John Foster, 1991. *Talking and Writing from Experience*, Macmillan English.
Copyright restrictions on p. ii.

▶ *First person narrative*

Midnight

Midnight may seem a pretty commonplace time to adult city dwellers. To a pair of eight-year-old boys in a small East Coast Scottish town the witching hour was just that – a time, we assumed, when everything would be transformed, would *feel* different, a time therefore that we were certainly not permitted to experience.

We resolved to see for ourselves just how alien midnight might be. For some reason (perhaps because he was a vital five months older) my friend David agreed to get up first and come the few doors to my house where the time-honoured device of a piece of string, which went from the garden all the way up to where it was tied to my big toe, would wake me up.

It worked! I dressed and silently joined David, who was standing shivering slightly in the shrubbery at the side of our garden. The streets were utterly deserted with that intense quiet which is so special and so rare in the middle of a town.

We walked a little way. We heard footsteps like footsteps you might hear in a thriller made in black and white at Ealing Studios. For this was the mid-1950s and, in retrospect, I remember those midnight streets in monochrome.

The steps were those of a policeman, the black and white check band round his cap just visible as we crouched behind a low garden wall. We waited some minutes and then began to realise that midnight meant nothingness – the removal of all the diversions of the day which made life interesting. We made for home, and said goodnight and I tiptoed up the steps for the front door. It was locked!

Momentary panic was controlled by the memory of the bathroom window – always open and accessible by climbing a wall and traversing a low roof. I had done it dozens of times in the day and was to use it frequently, returning late after teenage parties. On this first nocturnal climb the haven of the bathroom was reached in a few minutes.

Just as I closed the window I heard my parents' bedroom door open. I guiltily pulled the chain just as my father switched on the bathroom light and started back slightly as he saw me. 'Goodnight, Dad,' I said and slipped past as he rubbed his eyes blearily.

It seemed to take hours to get to sleep but I was not disturbed again. Over breakfast my father suddenly stopped eating and said, 'How strange, I had a sudden conviction that you had your clothes on when I came into the bathroom last night.' He shrugged his shoulders. I ate my porridge silently.

from 'Caught in the act', *an autobiographical article by Neil McIntosh*

● ●

Yr 8

TASK 2 First and third person narrative 1

Aim To compare first and third person narratives and to develop a short story based on a personal experience written either in the first person or the third person

Read Sasha Norton's short story (Sheet 34), loosely based on a personal experience, written in the first person.

ADAPTING THE IDEA

Sasha got the idea for her story after reading the story of a girl who borrowed a precious necklace from her mother and lost it. She remembered the time she broke a china cheetah of her mother's and decided to use the memory as the starting point for her story. But she decided to adapt the facts to suit the story as she wanted to tell it. In reality, it wasn't a friend who broke the cheetah, but Sasha herself and though her mother was fond of the gift, it wasn't a wedding present.

- In pairs, decide whether Sasha's story reminds you of a time when you broke or lost something belonging to someone else. Or of a time when you had done something wrong and were 'waiting for the awful moment to come'. Tell each other memories of similar incidents.

  Then, choose one of the incidents which could be used as the starting point for a story. Discuss together ways you could adapt the story. Be as inventive as you like. There is no need to stick to the facts. Alter them as much as you want in order to suit your idea for the story.

- Each write the first draft of a version of the story. One of you write the story in the first person, the other write it in the third person. Compare your drafts, decide whose version works best for your story and together redraft and produce a final version of the story.

- Continue Sasha's story. One of you describe her mother's return using a first person narrative, the other describe her return using a third person narrative. Afterwards, compare your different versions.

© Judith Atkinson and John Foster, 1991. *Talking and Writing from Experience*. Macmillan English.
Copyright restrictions on p. ii.

First and third person narrative 1

The Cheetah and the Rollerskate

The doorbell rang. I charged down the stairs and opened the door. There stood three grinning friends, Sam, Joanne and Tessa. 'Hi! Come in. Where's Nina?' I asked.

'She went shopping,' was Joanne's reply.

I liked it when the gang came round. We messed about, played stupid games and sometimes we cooked something. I silently hoped they wouldn't ask to cook anything, because the last time they came we set the cooker alight by an accident with some vegetable oil.

'Is anyone at home apart from you?' asked Sam.

'No,' I replied.

'Oh good. Can me and Joanne have a go on your video game?'

'Joanne and I!' corrected Tessa. (She had gone mad on proper English grammar, ever since she got told off by her teacher for speaking bad English.)

'Alright. Joanne and I. Better?' asked Sam.

'Hmm,' murmured Tessa.

By that time I had already plugged in the video and turned on the television. Sam and Joanne started playing the game and Tessa and I looked through an old fashion magazine.

After a while, Sam went into the kitchen to get some drinks. She poured out cokes and brought them in on a tray. As she came into the sitting-room, she noticed rollerskates. 'Hey, whose are these?' she asked. I knew what she was holding without even looking up from the magazine. I had put them down where someone would find them, easily, without looking too hard.

'They're mine. Good, aren't they?' I asked with pride.

'They're really good! Even better than mine!' said Sam. 'Can I try them out?' she asked.

'Yes, if you want to,' I replied.

'Catch,' said Sam. She whizzed the skate across the smooth, linoleum floor.

'What?' said Joanne, looking round from the game.

'Get the skate before it –' But it was too late. The skate thundered into the large china cheetah in the corner of the room. The rollerskate rebounded and a few fragments of china fell to the floor.

I couldn't believe it. The china cheetah, the precious cheetah, the wedding-gift cheetah, now the smashed cheetah.

At first, I was angry, then tears began to well in my eyes. I was ashamed of being so irresponsible.

Sam apologised and said she would get her money from the bank to pay for the repair of the cheetah. She started weeping, so Joanne took her home.

Tessa stayed with me for a while and we tidied up the room. 'I'll stay till your mum gets home, if you want,' offered Tessa.

'N-no, no thanks,' I managed to say between sobs. I rushed upstairs to my bedroom and locked myself in. I heard the outside door slam and I broke down and cried. I stayed there, crying, waiting for the awful moment to come.

Sasha Norton

TASK 3 *First and third person narrative 2*

Aim To consider further the use of first and third person narrative, using a personal experience of disappointment or surprise

The story *The miser* (Sheet 36) is based on the author's memories of preparations for a particular Bonfire Night. Instead, however, of writing in the first person David Lodge tells his story in the third person.

- In groups, talk about what happens in the story. Did the ending come as a surprise? Are there any clues in the way the story is told that enable you to predict the ending.

- Although the story is written in the third person, the focus is on the central character Timothy and his feelings. Discuss the different feelings Timothy experiences during the story and draw a chart or diagram showing how his feelings change.

- What difference would it make to the story if it had been written in the first person? Try rewriting the last section of the story in the first person, starting at 'On the evening of November 4th ...' Do you think the section is more or less effective when it is written in the first person? Say why.

- Prepare for a piece of writing of your own by sharing memories of times when you have looked forward to something but it has turned out to be bitterly disappointing, such as:

  going to a party or a disco; going on an outing or on holiday; taking part in a play, match or concert; Bonfire Night or some other festival or celebration; meeting someone you had always wanted to meet; being given the 'wrong' present

  and of times when you have had an unexpected pleasant surprise, such as:

  a new pet; an unexpected present; a visit from someone; getting chosen for something; winning a prize.

- On your own, choose a memory of a disappointment or a pleasant surprise to use as the starting point for a story. You can adapt the facts in any way you like. But don't make the story too far-fetched. The test of a good autobiographical story like this is to make it so convincing that the reader can't tell which parts actually happened and which parts you have made up.

  Before you begin, decide whether to write it in the first person or the third person.

First and third person narrative 2

The miser

After the War there was a terrible shortage of fireworks. During the War there hadn't been any fireworks at all; but that was because of the blackout, and because the fireworks-makers were making bombs instead. When the War ended everybody said all the pre-war things, like fireworks, would come back. But they hadn't.

Timothy's mother said the rationing was disgraceful, and his father said they wouldn't catch him voting Labour again, but fireworks weren't even rationed. Rationing would have been fair, anyway, even if it was only six each, or say twelve. Twelve different ones. But there just weren't any fireworks to be had, unless you were very lucky. Sometimes boys at school brought them in, and let off the odd banger in the bogs, for a laugh. They spoke vaguely of getting them 'down the Docks', or from a friend of their dad's, or from a shop that had discovered some pre-war stock, and sold out the same day.

Timothy and Drakey and Woppy had searched all over the neighbourhood for such a shop. Once they did find a place advertising fireworks, but when the man brought them out they were all the same kind, bangers. You couldn't have a proper Guy Fawkes' Night with just bangers. Besides, they weren't one of the proper makes, like Wells, Standard, or Payne's. They were called 'Whizzo', and had a suspiciously home-made look about them. They cost tenpence each, which was a shocking price to charge for bangers. In the end they bought two each and, with only three weeks to go before November 5th, that was still their total stock.

One day Timothy's mother set his heart leaping when she came in from shopping and announced that she had got some fireworks for him. But when she produced them they were only the sparkler things that you held in your hand – little kids' stuff. He'd been so sulky that in the end his mother wouldn't let him have the sparklers, which he rather regretted afterwards.

None of them, not even Drakey, who was the oldest, had a clear memory of Guy Fawkes' Night before the War. But they all remembered VJ Night, when there was a bonfire on the bomb-site in the middle of the street where the flying-bomb had fallen, and the sky was gaudy with rockets, and a man from one of the houses at the end of the street had produced two whole boxes of super fireworks, saying he'd saved them for six years for this night. The next morning Timothy had roamed the bomb-site and collected all the charred cases as, in previous years, he had collected shrapnel. That was when he had first learned the

First and third person narrative 2

The miser

haunting names – 'Chrysanthemum Fire', 'Roman Candle', 'Volcano', 'Silver Rain', 'Torpedo', 'Moonraker' – beside which the 'Whizzo Banger' struck a false and unconvincing note.

One Saturday afternoon Timothy, Drakey and Woppy wandered far from their home ground, searching for fireworks. The best kind of shop was the kind that sold newspapers, sweets, tobacco and a few toys. They found several new ones, but had no luck. Some of the shops even had notices in the window: 'No Fireworks'.

'If they had any,' said Drakey bitterly, 'I bet they wouldn't sell them. They'd keep them for their own kids.'

'Let's go home,' said Woppy. 'I'm tired.'

On the way home they played 'The Lost Platoon', a game based on a serial story in Drakey's weekly comic. Drakey was Sergeant McCabe, the leader of the platoon, Timothy was Corporal Kemp, the quiet, clever one, and Woppy was 'Butch' Baker, the strong but rather stupid private. The platoon was cut off behind enemy lines and the game consisted in avoiding the

First and third person narrative 2

The miser

observation of Germans. Germans were anyone who happened to be passing.

'Armoured vehicles approaching,' said Timothy.

Drakey led them into the driveway of a private golf course. They lay in some long grass while two women with prams passed on the pavement. Timothy glanced idly round him, and sat up sharply.

'Look!' he breathed, scarcely able to believe such luck. About thirty yards away, on some rough ground screened from the road by the golf-club fence, was a ramshackle wooden shed. Leaning against one wall was a notice, crudely painted on a wooden board. 'Fireworks for Sale,' it said.

Slowly they got to their feet and, with silent, wondering looks at each other, approached the shed. The door was open, and inside an old man was sitting at a table, reading a newspaper and smoking a pipe. A faded notice over his head said: 'Smoking Prohibited'. He looked up and took the pipe out of his mouth.

'Yes?' he said.

Timothy looked for help to Drakey and Woppy, but they were just gaping at the man and at the dusty boxes piled on the floor.

'Er . . . you haven't any fireworks, have you?' Timothy ventured at last.

'Yes, I've got a few left, son. Want to buy some?'

The fireworks were sold loose, not in pre-packed boxes, which suited them perfectly. They took a long time over their selection, and it was dark by the time they had spent all their money. On the way home they stopped under each lamp-post to open their paper bags and reassure themselves that their treasure was real. The whole episode had been like a dream, or a fairy tale, and Timothy was afraid that at any moment the fireworks would dissolve.

As they reached the corner of their street, Timothy said: 'Whatever you do, don't tell anybody where we got them.'

'Why?' said Woppy.

'So that we can go back and get some more, before he sells out.'

'I've spent all my fireworks money anyway,' said Drakey.

'Yes, but it's ages to Guy Fawkes, and we've got pocket money to come,' argued Timothy.

But when they went back the following Saturday, the shed was locked, and the notice was gone. They peered through the windows, but there was only dusty furniture to be seen.

'Must have sold out,' said Drakey. But there was something creepy about the sudden disappearance of the fireworks man, and

First and third person narrative 2

The miser

they hurried away from the shed and never spoke of it again.

Each evening, as soon as he got home from school, Timothy got out the box in which he had put his fireworks and counted them. He took them all out and arranged them, first according to size, then according to type, then according to price. He pored over the brightly-coloured labels, studying intently the blurred instructions: *hold in a gloved hand, place in earth and stand well back, nail to a wooden post*. He handled the fireworks with great care, grudging every grain of gunpowder that leaked out and diminished the glory to come.

'I wonder you keep those things under your bed,' said his mother. 'Remember what happened to the sweets.'

About a year previously, an American relative had sent Timothy a large box of 'candies', as she called them. Their bright wrappings and queer names – *Oh Henry!*, *Lifesavers* and *Baby Ruth* – had fascinated him much as the fireworks did; and he was so overwhelmed by the sense of his own wealth amid universal sweet-rationing that he had hoarded them under his bed and ate them sparingly. But they had started to go mouldy, and attracted mice, and his mother threw them away.

'Mice don't eat fireworks,' he said to her, stroking the stick of his largest rocket. But on second thoughts, he asked his mother to keep them for him in a warm, dry cupboard.

'How d'you know they'll go off, anyway?' said his father. 'Pre-war, aren't they? Probably dud by now.'

Timothy knew his father was teasing, but he took the warning seriously. 'We'll have to try one,' he said solemnly to Drakey and Woppy, 'To see if they're all right. We'd better draw lots.'

'I don't mind letting off one of mine,' said Drakey.

'No, I want to let off one of mine,' said Woppy.

In the end, they let off one each. Woppy chose a 'Red Flare', and Drakey a 'Roman Candle'. Timothy couldn't understand why they didn't let off the cheapest ones. They went to the bomb-site to let them off. For a few dazzling seconds the piles of rubble, twisted iron, planks and rusty water cisterns were illuminated with garish colour. When it was over they blinked in the dim light of the street-lamps and grinned at each other.

'Well, they work all right,' said Drakey.

The other two tried to persuade Timothy to let off one of his. He was tempted, but he knew he would regret it later, and refused. They quarrelled, and Drakey taunted Timothy with being a Catholic like Guy Fawkes. Timothy said that he didn't care, that you didn't have to be against Guy Fawkes to have

▶ *First and third person narrative 2*

The miser

fireworks, and that he wasn't interested in the Guy part anyway. He went home alone, got out his fireworks, and sat in his bedroom all the evening, counting and arranging them.

Once Drakey and Woppy had broken into their store, they could not restrain themselves till November 5th. They started with one firework a night, then it went up to two, then it was three. Drakey had a talent for discovering new and spectacular ways of using them. He would drop a lighted banger into an old water tank and produce an explosion that brought the neighbours to their doors, or he would shoot a 'Torpedo' out of a length of drain-pipe. Timothy had a few ideas of his own, but, as he stubbornly refused to use any of his own fireworks, the most he could ask was to be a passive spectator. His turn would come on November 5th, when the empty-handed Drakey and Woppy would be glad to watch his display.

On the evening of November 4th, Timothy counted his collection for the last time.

'You'll be lost without those things after tomorrow,' said his mother.

'I don't believe he really wants to set them off,' said his father.

''Course I do,' said Timothy. But he closed the lid of the box with a sigh.

'I'll be glad to see the back of them, anyway,' said his mother. 'Now, who could that be?'

His father answered the door. The policeman was so big he seemed to fill the entire room. He smiled encouragingly at Timothy, but Timothy just hugged his box to his chest, and looked at his feet.

'Look, Sergeant,' said his father, 'I realise that if these fireworks are really stolen goods –'

'Not exactly stolen, sir,' said the policeman, 'But as good as. This old codger just broke into the storage shed and set up shop.'

'Well, what I mean is, I know you're entitled to take them away, but this is a special case. You know what kids are like about fireworks. He's been looking forward to Guy Fawkes' Night for weeks.'

'I know, sir, I've got kids myself. But I'm sorry. This is the only lot we've been able to trace. We'll need them for evidence.' He turned to Timothy. 'D'you happen to know, sonny, if any of your friends bought fireworks off the same man?'

Timothy nodded speechlessly, trying not to cry. 'But I'm the only one that saved them,' he said: and with the words the tears rolled uncontrollably down his cheeks.

David Lodge

40 ●

YR 7

Diary writing

Aim To write a number of diary entries in which you describe your thoughts and feelings

- In pairs, read the entries from Moira Andrew's diary on Sheets 42 and 43. How is the style of a diary entry different from the style of a piece of narrative prose? Pick out some examples.

  Each choose a different paragraph from the diary and rewrite it, as you would if it were part of a first person narrative story. Then, show each other what you have written, discuss the changes you have made and why you made them.

- On your own, think of a day which you remember clearly for some reason – a birthday, the first time you went to spend a night away from home on your own, a day you spent in bed, a day you spent in hospital, a day when you did something for the very first time.

  Write a diary entry like Moira Andrew's in which you describe the day in detail. As well as describing what happened, include comments and asides which say what you were thinking and feeling. It can be funny or sad – as long as it's entertaining!

- Keep a diary for a week. Instead of writing it for yourself, write it to be read by someone who lives in another part of the country, or in another country. Select things to record in your diary that will give the reader a clear idea of you, the life you lead, your interests, your thoughts and feelings – about school, your home, the place you live, the things you do in your free time.

  You could put your diary entries on to a computer, produce a booklet and send it to a school in another part of the country for people of your own age to read. Don't forget to ask them to send their diary entries for you to read!

YR 7

Diary writing

Monday, 3rd April

Woke up covered in spots. Looked like a leopard, and Dad called me The Lesser Spotted Tree Toad. Harry said he didn't know about the Lesser bit and did you get More Spotted Tree Toads? Brothers! Mum said, 'Just you wait, my boy. It's only a matter of time.'

Had to stay off school. Spots itch like anything. Mum put some pink lotion on them. Felt better after that, but looked like an iced bun with cherries on top. Fell asleep for a while – ever so funny in the middle of the morning with the sun shining in. Thought about them all doing maths and workbooks and things at school. Remembered that today's the day Miss Warner said she would pick the netball team. Hope she doesn't forget about me.

Sat up in bed and played with paper dolls. Did some drawing but Mum wasn't too pleased when I got red felt-tip on the sheet. Read my books for a long time. Got fed up. Called for Mum. She came chasing upstairs shouting, 'Run to the bathroom if you feel sick.' Said I wasn't sick, just bored. 'It's only 11 o'clock,' Mum said. 'You've a lot of day to go, so you'd better find something to do.' Couldn't believe it was just after break. Felt like home-time.

Had a drink of juice. Looked at the spots on the back of my hands. One is like old Mr Feather's Morris Minor. If you look at it another way it's a toadstool or an anchor or a shark. A bit like clouds. They can be anything you want them to be. Miss Warner always says I've got a good imagination.

Doorbell rang. Grandma! A visitor at last. She brought me some fizzy yellow stuff to drink. Didn't like it much, but I drank it to please her. Grandma taught me to play Gin Rummy which sounds very grand. She told me about having Scarlet Fever when she was a little girl. They sprayed the whole house and all her clothes with some smelly disinfectant. Then they took her off to hospital for three weeks! Hope that doesn't happen to me, but Grandma said that was in the Old Days.

Had lunch in bed. Mum made me chicken sandwiches with the

Diary writing

crusts cut off. She called them chickenpox sandwiches and Grandma said chicken-spots sandwiches and I said chicken-socks sandwiches and we all laughed like anything. Mum said, 'That's enough nonsense. You'll get all hot and bothered again.' They had lunch on a tray in my bedroom and it was like a tea party. Had raspberry yoghurt for afters – my favourite! Yummy. Decided that chickenpox wasn't too bad after all.

Life got boring again after Grandma left. Spots started to itch again. More pink lotion. More juice. Another sleep. Woke to hear Harry throwing his schoolbag down, banging the front door and shouting that he was back home! A waste of time. Nobody could miss him. He came storming upstairs to ask how the Greater Mottled Pond Frog was doing. Very funny! Just wait till he gets it – in about three weeks Mum says.

He gave me a letter from Miss Warner. I'm in the team! Wow! And she says she hopes I'll be better soon and that they all miss me. Harry called me Teacher's Pet, so we had a row. Mum called up, 'Stop that this minute, you two! Come downstairs or you'll miss Blue Peter.' Watched TV in my dressing-gown.

Dad came home and said he'd had a brute of a day and wasn't I lucky having a whole day to laze about in bed. I said it was boring and Dad said that was impossible with all the things I had to play with. Then Harry started to have a go at me. Mum said, 'Leave the poor girl alone. Can't you see she's ill.' Felt very important.

Had an early bath and was quite glad to go back to bed. Dad came up and read a bit of The Hobbit. Mum and Harry came in and listened too. Dad's got a terrific voice. He should be on the stage or a news-reader on Breakfast Television. Told him so. He was very surprised and said that it was his secret ambition. Imagine that!

Didn't feel tired. All that sleeping in the day-time. Listened to the downstairs sounds of TV and Mum and Dad laughing. Watched the sky grow dark. Saw the first pale stars. Looked like the sky had chickenpox too!

Moira Andrew

TASK 2 — Reflective writing

YR 7

Aim To talk and write about your life, reflecting on your home life and your relationships with the people you live with

Maria, aged fourteen, and Tariq, aged fifteen, have each written about their family, reflecting on relationships within the family (Sheets 45 and 46).

- Maria's teacher commented that she had written 'objectively', standing outside herself and looking thoughtfully at the way her relationship with her parents was changing as she grew up.

  Working in pairs, go through her essay carefully and pick out the comments which show Maria reflecting about her relationship with her parents.

- Look at each paragraph of Maria's writing in turn. Discuss what she says in it. Compare it to your own experiences. How similar/different are your relationships with the adults you live with?

- Like Maria, Tariq writes objectively about his family. What do you learn about his father, his mother and his sisters from his account of his family background? Draw a chart and list what he tells you about each member of his family.

- What does Tariq tell you about himself in his essay? What is his attitude to his 'strange situation'?

- On your own, think carefully and note down some ideas about the way your attitude has changed towards other people as you have grown up. Think about

    the adults in your family   friends
    sisters and/or brothers   teachers.

- Then, think about and jot down ideas about the way your attitude has changed towards things you took for granted as a young child e.g. television, clothes, food, festivals and celebrations, the environment, money, music, schoolwork, your free time, the future.

- Now, like Maria and Tariq, try to explore your thoughts in writing. Begin by looking through your notes and make a plan by numbering the points in the order you are going to make them. You needn't stick rigidly to the plan, but it should help you to put your thoughts in order. Give your reflections a title, such as 'Growing up', 'How my life has changed' or 'My family life'.

Reflective writing

Growing up

For all fourteen years of my life I have lived with my Mum and Dad, reasonably happily. Arguments arise fairly often between us, but they don't usually result in much. I can beat my Mum occasionally in an argument but with my Dad, very rarely.

My Mum and Dad are really out of date when it comes to modern music. It really gets me mad when I am listening to the 'top 40' on a Sunday and my Dad sits in the same room, passing comments about what he does or doesn't think about the modern music scene, but in the mornings when we have his Radio 2 on, with Gladys Knight and the Pips blaring out, my Dad will get in a mood and say something like, 'What a flipping noise, what do we have to listen to this rubbish for?' But if I ask to put Radio 1 on he nearly hits the roof and a few words fly.

My Mum always thinks that she knows best, including when it comes to my money. When I have a bit of money put to one side, my Mum suddenly becomes very good at deciding what I need. The only way to stop my Mum helping spend my money is to hide it, so she never knows how much money I have got.

'Worrywart' must be my Mum's middle name, she never stops worrying. She likes to give me as much freedom as I want, but when she gives me her consent to stay out late, she never stops worrying until I am home.

I don't like to confide my secrets in my Mum, because she would just tell my Dad. My Mum is usually quite understanding, but when it comes to boys she doesn't always understand. If I say I really like someone, she lectures me on not getting too serious. So I prefer not to tell my parents when I am seeing someone. I'm glad I can ring my brother and confide in him, he understands.

My only real complaint against my parents is that I wish they were a bit more understanding and took a bit more notice of me, now my brother is away from home.

Maria

Reflective writing

Two cultures – one person

I'm in a kind of strange situation. I feel different to most other people because my father is from Pakistan and my mother is from Italy.

My father is now 56 years old and has been living in this country for 28 years. He is a serious man but he has a good sense of humour, he has lots of friends from many different cultures.

My mother is 46 years old and moved to England when she was 21. My parents say that it was 'love at first sight'. At first they used to see each other secretly, but when the Auntie found out she was strongly against the idea because of my father's race. My mother's family ordered her back to Italy. My father wrote letters to my mother in Italy, but her family tried to stop her receiving them.

Eventually, my mother booked a flight from Italy and came over to see my father. When her family found out they demanded to meet him. When they did, they liked him and agreed that the marriage could go ahead. They were married in a Catholic Church and all the family from Italy came over.

Once married, they went on to have three children. Ahsia is the oldest, she is now 17. Ahsia was named after my father's mother. She goes to College, works hard at her studies and plans to go to University. She doesn't go out much because my father is very strict with her.

My younger sister is 14 years old and also works hard at her studies. She won a prize for drawing a summer picture and appeared in the local evening paper. Everyone was very proud of her. She does not go out much either because my dad is also strict with her.

My sisters do not wear skirts because Muslims are not allowed to show their legs. They are restricted from doing a lot of things and my sisters, with my mother, always argue with father about this. I stay out of it but they always manage to compromise in the end.

I am 15 years old, I don't work that hard at school and I have been in a fair bit of trouble. My father keeps telling me to work harder. I am hardly ever at home but my father is very sexist and he says that a man can take care of himself more easily than a woman.

All three children are Muslims. We do not eat meat unless it is Halal, which I think means that it has been prayed over during its preparation. We also don't drink alcohol. We do not know much about the religion because none of us can speak or understand the Pakistani language. We do not celebrate Eid but we always celebrate Christmas. We buy each other presents and have lots of fun.

A lot of people ask me what nationality I am and when I tell them, they all seem surprised and start asking questions such as: what food do you eat? I tell them I eat both kinds, Pakistani and Italian, my mother can make both. Then people ask things like: which nationality would you rather be? I reply by saying that I am happy the way I am and that I am proud of both cultures.

Tariq

YR 7

A reading journal

Aim To keep a reading journal in which you record your responses to the books you read

There are a number of ways of keeping a reading journal.

- **While you are reading**
  You can keep a journal, as Sithu (Sheet 50) does, recording your responses to a book while you are reading it. The advantages of doing this are that it helps you to develop your ability to think critically about a book throughout your reading of it and not only when you have finished it.

  When you stop to make an entry, write down your thoughts and feelings about:

  1 *Incidents in the book.* How do you feel about what has happened? Have any parts of the plot disappointed you? Can you predict what is going to happen?

  2 *Ideas in the book.* How interesting is the book's theme? Have any parts of the book made you realise something new or made you think? Have any parts of the book reminded you of thoughts or experiences of your own?

  3 *Characters in the book.* What do you think about the choices they have made and the things they have done? Would you have acted as they did? How do you feel about them – do you admire or dislike any of them? Why?

- **After reading**
  You can summarise your responses to a book, by writing comments after you have read it, as Lisa (Sheet 48) does. Before you start writing, use the headings and questions above to help you to clarify your thoughts and feelings.

- **Questions and answers**
  You can review your responses to a book by thinking up a series of questions for someone to ask you about the book, then getting them to interview you about it. You can tape-record your answers and then record them in your journal, like Justine (Sheet 49) did.

- **Group discussions**
  A group of you, who have read the same book, can discuss the plot, characters, themes and issues raised. You can keep notes during the discussion, then write a summary of your own and other people's responses in your journal.

A reading journal

Here are Lisa's comments after reading two novels.

My thoughts about
DEAR AMANDA

This was a Sweet Dreams romance book recommended by my friends. It was the classic love story: boy likes girl, girl likes boy, but neither will admit it. They eventually come together through 'Dear Amanda'.

For a Sweet Dreams romance this was quite readable. It was funny and I found myself sympathising with the girl behind 'Dear Amanda', but it was boring at the same time because I knew the ending as soon as all the characters had been introduced.

I don't often read books like this, but this was one of the funnier ones. I prefer 'different', unsuspected endings, instead of all the books being exactly the same but with different names.

My thoughts about
THE GROWING PAINS OF
ADRIAN MOLE

This is the second diary belonging to Adrian Mole – it is just as witty and you can relate to the problems Adrian goes through. I saw this on TV before I read it, so my imagination couldn't work as well, as I remembered the scenes and the actors. This spoiled it a bit. I've also just read The Diary of a Teenage Health Freak which was more or less the same thing, but more informative. It's clever the way the diaries are written. You must have to get right inside the character to capture the way he or she thinks.

A reading journal

After reading *Summer of my German Soldier* by Betty Greene, Justine recorded an interview in which her partner asked her questions about her reactions to the novel. Justine then wrote up the interview in her journal. This is part of it.

How did Patty get on with her family?
Her parents obviously favoured her younger sister, Sharon, because she's pretty and to them acts how a young girl should, but they only seem to notice Patty when she's doing something wrong – this is especially true of her father.

What was their relationship like?
Well, at first I thought Harry Bergen hated Patty because of his aggressive and totally uninterested attitude towards her, but later on I decided it was more complicated than that. Patty does annoy him a lot, but you can tell when you're reading that she doesn't mean to do it. She tries desperately to impress him – like when she buys him an expensive shirt for Father's Day – but then is disappointed again when he hardly seems to notice it. That's one of the ways Anton, the soldier, is different, because when Patty gave the shirt to him he even stopped to examine the special buttons.

So why does her father treat her like that?
I think Patty and her father were on different wavelengths: they were trying to reach each other but they couldn't. I think he was really looking for something to be proud of Patty about, because she wasn't pretty like Sharon, but maybe he was looking in the wrong places. That's why he almost seemed to disown her in the end.

▶ *A reading journal*

Here are the comments Sithu made on *Whispering in the wind* by Alan Marshall, as he was reading.

AFTER THE FIRST THREE CHAPTERS
The story so far has started well – I'm finding it exciting. It could be improved, though, by introducing pictures of the various scenes and what the main characters look like. The author does drop hints to make you imagine but I'd still like to know more.

AFTER CHAPTER 8
I now think the plot is original with some strange experiences for Peter in his quest. It seems that the magic leaf Peter gives to people he meets turns enemies or hostile creatures into friends.

AFTER FINISHING THE BOOK
I now feel that the two heroes, Peter and Greyfur, are almost too perfect and the author has made the enemies no match for them – in fact, they're easy to overcome. I thought the journey across Australia would have more exciting dangers in it but their worst experiences were being exhausted from travelling. I also thought at first that Alan Marshall didn't describe things enough, now it seems that he sometimes spoils a very good idea with too much description.

Yr 6

Letters to a penfriend

Aim To write a letter to a new penfriend introducing yourself.

- In pairs, before reading Judith's letter to her new penfriend (Sheet 52), make a checklist of all the information you would include in a letter to a new penfriend.

- Now read Judith's letter. Does it include all the information you put on your checklist? What other information, if any, has she included? Do you think she has included any unnecessary information?

- Below is the draft of another letter of introduction. Discuss it with your partner and decide what advice you would give to Jane about how to redraft her letter to improve its content and its organisation. Then, join up with another pair and compare the advice you would give her.

> Dear Francoise
>
> I was born in October 1978 at the local hospital. I was christened Jane Elizabeth Earl. One of my aunties is my godmother. My godfather is my dad's brother and my other godmother is my mum's best friend.
>
> We have lived in my present house all my life. I have one brother whose name is David. He can be very annoying. I have been abroad five times, four times to Spain and once to Italy. I have never been to France. I love nearly all animals and I myself have a dog called Shep. He is an Alsatian.
>
> I enjoy most of school life, but there are a few exceptions. I enjoy writing stories in English and I spend a lot of time reading because the youth club is only open for juniors on Tuesdays and Fridays.
>
> Please write and tell me what you are like.
>
> Yours sincerely
>
> *Jane Earl*
>
> JANE EARL

- On your own, study the advertisements giving details of people who are looking for a penfriend (Sheet 53). Choose one of them and write a letter introducing yourself to her/him. In your letter, use the facts you know about the person to whom you are writing and make some comparisons between your life and her/his life.

Letters to a penfriend

Here is a letter written by a 12-year-old girl to her new penfriend.

65 Thames Street,
Southwold,
Worcestershire
5th May

Dear Vicky,

I am so pleased that you want to be my penfriend. How old are you? I am twelve nearly thirteen. I have one brother and sister. My brother's name is Robert and he is seventeen. My sister's name is Alison and she is fifteen. We're nearly always squabbling. Have you any brothers or sisters? My mother is a teacher, luckily she doesn't teach at my school!

I have quite a few pets. My sister has a rabbit called Tosca; she had six quite unexpected babies. I have got a rat called Fizzy. Do you like rats? I like domestic rats (Fizzy is one of these) but I don't like wild rats. Fizzy had six babies a week after I got her! She is very, very tame.

My sister and I share a baby guinea-pig called Cherry. She's not very tame at the moment, for we haven't had her very long. My whole family and I share a cat called Geoffrey – he's six years old. Have you got any pets?

I live in a town called Southwold; it's a very nice place. It is a market town and has been for a long time. There are a lot of old buildings in Southwold. What's your town like?

I have quite a few hobbies. I love sport, especially netball, swimming and rounders. I also like reading. I have singing and piano lessons and hope to be learning another instrument soon. I expect you have got a lot of hobbies too.

Do you watch much television? I do sometimes. My favourite programme is a comedy serial called 'Happy Days'. Do you know it? The main character in it is a man called 'Fonz'. This programme is very silly and funny.

I go to school in Southwold. It's a comprehensive school. We start in the morning at 8.50 and stop at 3.45 in the afternoon. I quite enjoy school. Do you?

About once every year I go to Scotland to see my aunt and uncle and my three cousins. They live in a town called Gateport, which is a lovely place.

My oldest cousin is Lewis and he is seven. Philip is four and Max is nearly two. Near Gateport is a fantastic beach called Shinkiddy. There's nothing but miles of sand and sea. One day in April last year I actually had a swim. I was the only person to do so. It was very cold indeed!

This holiday is my favourite and I look forward to it every year. Have you got a favourite holiday too?

Please write soon and tell me all about yourself.

Love,
Judith

▶ Letters to a penfriend

NAME Fraser Black   AGE 13
HOME Rochester, New York State, USA
FAMILY Father works at a sports centre
        Mother is a teacher
        Gran lives with us
INTERESTS AND HOBBIES Photography; computers; reading; films;
        skateboarding
LIKES Going fishing on holiday; horror films; Chinese food
DISLIKES People who talk too much; swimming; coffee

NAME Rosa Andreyev   AGE 14
HOME Moscow, USSR
FAMILY Father – engineer in a factory
        Mother – doctor
        1 brother – 16
INTERESTS AND HOBBIES Swimming; playing the clarinet; skiing; rock music
LIKES McDonalds; speaking English; watching TV; Sundays in the country
DISLIKES Queues; wet days in the city; my brother and his friends teasing
        me

NAME Pierre Armand   AGE 15
HOME Village near Marseilles, France
FAMILY Mother – writes children's books
        Sister – 20 (at university); brother – 14
        2 dogs; several hens and ducks
INTERESTS AND HOBBIES Jazz dance; soccer; collecting posters; 'green'
        issues
LIKES Talking on the telephone; clothes; soap operas
DISLIKES People who don't care about the environment; silence; maths

TASK 2 *Letters giving information*

Aim To write a letter giving instructions about how to get somewhere

Here is a letter from Rachel to her friend Sarah, who is coming to stay, giving her instructions how to find her way to their caravan.

Lot 3
Hornbeach Campsite
Hornbeach
August 3rd 1991

Dear Sarah,
I'm glad your parents have agreed to let you come to the caravan for the weekend. It's in the campsite near the cliffs so we'll be able to go down to the beach, as long as it's fine.

You said in your letter that your Dad will be bringing you in the car. This is how to find our caravan. There's a crossroads in the middle of Hornbeach village, just after the Spar supermarket. Turn right there, following the sign 'To the sea'. The road is narrow and winding once you've left the village. After a big left bend you'll see the ruin of an old lighthouse on your right and a row of four bungalows. Turn right just after the bungalows down a lane which is signposted 'Hornbeach Campsite'. As soon as you've turned into the lane you'll be able to see the sea. The entrance to the site is a short way along on the left. Our caravan is the third on the right and has a sign on the door with our name on it.

Mum has asked me to say that she'll have lunch ready for 12.30! I'm looking forward to seeing you. Don't forget to bring your swimming things.

Love,

Rachel

Letters giving information

- How easy is it to follow Rachel's instructions? Imagine that Rachel included a sketch map with her letter. Draw the map of Hornbeach, marking in all the landmarks that Rachel mentions in her letter.

- Imagine that a friend is coming to stay with you. Their car has broken down, so s/he will have to come by public transport, getting a train to the station nearest to your home. Write a letter giving instructions on how to catch a bus from the station to your home.

- You have got tickets for a concert at your local theatre. A cousin who lives fifty miles away is coming to the concert because her favourite group are playing. Write a letter to her telling her how to get from either the bus station or the railway station to the theatre and explaining where you will meet her and what time you will meet her.

- An author is coming to talk to your class about the books she writes. She lives an hour's drive away from the school. She will be travelling by car and needs to know how to reach your school from either the motorway, the ring road or the town centre, whichever is nearest. Write a letter to her explaining how to get to the school and where to park her car when she arrives.

TASK 3 In my opinion

Aim To write a letter expressing your opinion on an issue which you feel is important

- In groups, study the five letters which were written to a newspaper for young people. Imagine you had to choose one of the letters to win a £10 prize as Letter of the Week. Which letter would you choose and why?

  Some points to consider:

  Which letter has the most effective opening?

  In which letter is the main statement best supported by the arguments developed and the evidence quoted?

  Which letter has the most effective ending?

  Which letter involves the reader most effectively?

  Prepare a statement to present to the rest of the class explaining your choice. Comment on the strengths and weaknesses of all the letters, not just the one you choose as the winner.

- What did you learn from studying the letters about how to structure and organise, and what style to use in, letters expressing opinions? Talk about and list any similarities a) in the way the letters start, develop and end b) in the types of sentences the writers use and the ways in which they try to involve the reader.

- Each draft a letter to a newspaper like *Early Times* or *The Indy* expressing your opinion on an issue that you think is important. (You could do this on a computer, then print out enough copies for each member of the group to have a copy.) Then, read each other's letters and discuss how effective they are. Choose one letter to be your group's Letter of the Week.

In my opinion

Circus animals

IN LAST WEEK'S issue you quoted from a book which suggests that the majority of circus animals are well looked after and that they actually enjoy being trained to perform.

I'm sure they *are* well cared for, but the whole idea of animals performing to entertain humans is unnatural and undignified.

Being part of a travelling circus also means that animals are kept cooped up in tiny cages. If they were really being well cared for, they would be roaming freely in large enclosures.

The best things about the traditional circus – the clowns, trapeze artists, jugglers – feature in modern circuses, which don't use performing animals at all. Let's encourage more of this and continue to enjoy seeing animals in their natural environment, behaving in a natural way.

Chris Fairbright, 14

Biker friendly?

I HAVE RECENTLY bought a bike and plan to cycle to school and to see friends.

As a 'new' cyclist, I am shocked by how badly we are treated in this country. Drivers, especially lorry drivers, cut you up, or behave as if they can't see you. Last week I was nearly knocked off my bike by a container lorry which pulled out without looking or signalling.

In other countries in Europe they have bicycle lanes everywhere. Why can't we do the same in Britain? Bicycles are the most environmentally friendly form of transport there is. If the government encouraged people to cycle, there'd be less pollution from traffic fumes and it would help the economy. Perhaps the Minister of Transport could set an example by cycling to work.

Donna, 14

Crazy crazes

WHY, OH WHY, do people fall for all these crazes! Last year it was all Kylie and Jason. Now it's Teenage Mutant Hero Turtles.

Don't they realise that these crazes are just packaged by marketing men? How about a bit of individuality for a change? I for one am going to go out and start a craze of my own. How about Plastic Monster Cockroaches?

Tom, 12

Rubbish

RECENTLY I HAD a holiday in Canada. The thing that struck me most about the country is that even in the main cities there is no litter accumulating in the gutters.

People say they are worried about the environment. If they really cared, they wouldn't drop their litter or throw it out of their car windows.

And another thing, why can't we arrange it so that different types of rubbish are collected separately? If paper, glass and cans were put out in separate containers, then they could be recycled.

We ought to do something, before it's too late.

Tina Russell, 13

Sun tans

I RECENTLY WENT on holiday with my family and was shocked at the lengths some people will go to to get a sun tan.

You lie around all day getting hot, sweaty and extremely uncomfortable. You can't move in case you miss that extra second of sun – you can't even read a book or magazine for fear of keeping one tiny bit of sun from your face or getting sun tan oil on it.

You end up looking like a boiled lobster and feeling extremely sore, unable to sleep at night because you have third degree burns on your back.

And what happens after all this self-inflicted torture? You go brown for about two days, then your skin starts to peel off in yucky flaky bits, which fall in your food and clog your clothes and your bed like old insect skins.

One of my black friends thinks it's really strange the lengths white people go to to be brown like her, especially when they make racist comments about people with skin colours different from their own.

It's a funny world!

From a reformed sunbather.

Kim Morris, 15

Yr 6

Describing places and scenes

Aim To write descriptions of places and scenes to give a picture of what your school is like.

Study the pieces of writing by Rachel, Samantha and Giles on Sheet 59.

- In groups, look at each description and decide how the writer has chosen to make you picture the scene.
- Each choose the description you prefer and explain to the rest of the group why you prefer it.
- On your own, write three or four descriptions of places in your school to help new pupils to picture them before they arrive.

  To help them to imagine the places, include in your descriptions what you can see, hear, feel and smell as well as what is going on and how people are moving, talking and acting. Make your descriptions short, but full of details, like snapshots.

  Here are some places and scenes you could describe: assembly, tutor period, the bike sheds, the changing rooms, the gym, a science lab, the changeover between lessons, the dining room, the computer room, out on the field on a wet day, the library, the end of the afternoon.

Describing places and scenes

Dinner Time

The bell has rung.
It's twelve o'clock – dinner time!
Classroom doors burst open.
Hungry faces down the corridor run to line up.
Trays are piled with food,
Stomachs rumble, eye balls roll.
Sandwiches, toad in the hole, chips and beans.
Lovely grub!
At the counter sits a lady with a rolling pin.
If you're noisy she'll bang on the table,
And shout.
Pay your money, find a table,
At last – dinner!

Rachel

A French Lesson

I enter the green and white tiled French room. People are talking and getting their books out. The French teacher enters and the room goes quiet, people rush back to their seats. The French teacher walks to his table.

'Ce la combien jodvie?' he says (or something like that). No hands are raised for the answer.

'Ohhhhhhhh. You sit there like suet puddings!' he shouts.

Somebody raises a hand and replies.

'C'est mercredi le 20 janvier.'

'Bravo, bravo! Très bien,' (thump, thump) the French teacher thumps the table, pleased.

'Alors, some writing.' There is a rustling noise as people turn to the backs of their books and get out their pens as fast as they can. Then they listen, concentrating hard on what the teacher is saying and occasionally writing answers.

Giles

English Room

Our English Room is also our dining room. It has a door at the front on the left and next to it is a blackboard with a pinboard around it with people's work on it. Next to that is a cupboard which is painted white and the handle is broken off. The walls are a peachy colour. At the back opposite the cupboard is a serving hatch with a grid coming down. The floor is tiled, the tiles are a creamy colour but there is also a pattern of red ones. The desks are an orangey-red colour and are like big tables. Smells of food drift into the room from the kitchen at the back. There are the sounds of people talking as they work. You can hear pens scribbling away and the pots and pans banging as the cooks move about the kitchen as they get the dinner ready. The teacher's heels are clicking around the room. As I look out of the window I can see the other block and people moving about in other classrooms. Seagulls are swooping down and there's wind in the trees.

Samantha

TASK
2 Yr 8

Describing experiences

Aim To write an account telling the story of a memorable event or events that you have experienced at school

- One of the best ways of helping strangers to feel what life is like in another school is to put them in your place: to show them what it is like through *your* experience. Read Naomi's story *A ghoul* (Sheet 61) then form groups and discuss these questions:

  1 What impression does Naomi give of her art project and her art teacher?

  2 Which of these statements sums up most accurately Naomi's attitude towards her art project?

    A She was very involved in the project and found it interesting.

    B She thought it was a good laugh.

    C She was enthusiastic at first, then gradually lost interest.

    D She couldn't care less about it.

    E She was disappointed because the project was less successful than she had hoped.

- One reader commented: 'Naomi succeeds in capturing the reader's attention and tells the story in an entertaining way.' Do you agree? Give your reasons.

- What are the most memorable things that have happened in your lessons during the last year? Share some of your memories that you could use as the basis for a piece of writing.

- Write the story of one of the memorable things that has happened to you at school this year. For example: the first day at school; when the science experiment went wrong; your class play; the day the team won! (or lost...); your day out; or anything memorable that has happened in or out of class.

  Remember it's important to help your reader picture the parts of the school you mention, your friends, your teachers, the conversations you had, as well as your thoughts and feelings on that day.

- Choose another incident that's happened to you at school and write it up in script form as though you were going to make an episode of a television serial based on *your* school instead of a fictional school like Grange Hill.

Describing experiences

A ghoul

'That is the most ugly and revolting item of creative art I think I've ever seen,' exclaimed Mrs Tailor admiringly. She removed her mauve-framed spectacles, and we stepped back from our creation with pride as she proceeded to examine some of its better aspects. We had known from the start that she would fall for Albert's captivating appearance, and the four of us mentally patted ourselves on the back.

As soon as Mrs Tailor had announced at the beginning of the Autumn term that for the next few weeks our art lessons would be conducted on the theme of 'Scary monster' we had hit upon the enterprising idea of constructing a titanic apparition out of cardboard boxes and other miscellaneous items of junk, instead of the mundane painted efforts the others in the class seemed content with producing.

After a full half-term of loving labour we now presented the finished product to Mrs Tailor: a peculiar assortment of cardboard boxes about three metres long and a metre high, with a disproportionately long toilet-roll neck supporting a pink egg-box mouth which gaped grotesquely open, displaying several rows of polystyrene teeth, enough to give a dentist nightmares. Its silver-foil eyes, although slightly out of alignment, still managed to glare balefully out upon the world in general. The ridiculously long neck was jammed into one of the eight large boxes constituting the body, which was supported by seven squat cake-box legs. The overall effect of menacing evil was somewhat spoiled by the fact that the putrid green paint which had been sloshed liberally over our abomination had failed to obscure the homely inscriptions, 'Spiller's Kattomeat' and 'Robinson's Whole-fruit Drinks', from his mighty torso.

Also, we had, to save clearing away after a lesson, stuck all the remains of our building materials onto his body at random, and the nasty rash of bright orange and green lentils and split-peas we had liberally applied to enhance our creation's supposedly wicked character had spread a rather gluey mess onto all the surrounding desks for some strange reason. This rather mouldered collection of dustbin-fodder was what we proudly christened 'Albert'.

Mrs Tailor finished her inspection of our monumental masterpiece, and remarked cautiously, 'He's very . . . er . . . cleverly made, but, well . . . just a little too big for us to keep. I have serious doubts as to whether he'd even fit through the door.' She smiled feebly at our outraged looks, and went on tactfully to suggest that we 'dismantle' him and start another piece of work.

Within a half-hour we formed a committee to discuss the homicide of the unfortunate Albert, and after many rather tempting suggestions of 'chucking him in the river' or 'burying him', systematic demolition was eventually favoured. Subsequently, Albert was unceremonially dismembered, jumped on, and finally cremated in an old dustbin in a decidedly unfunereal atmosphere.

Naomi

Yr 7

TASK 3 *Explaining and informing*

Aim To write an explanation of some of the basic information that a new pupil needs to know when s/he starts at your school

Here is a letter from a primary school pupil to a First Year at secondary school:

> Dear First Year pupil,
>
> I am coming to your school in September. Please could you answer the following questions?
>
> > Do you ever get bullied, and if you do where do you run to?
> > Do you get lost, and if you do what happens to you?
> > If you forget your homework, what happens?
> > Have you ever been caned?
> > Does it ever seem longer at secondary school than it does at junior school?
> >
> > > *Lisa*

- In groups, start by trying to answer Lisa's questions for your school. Then, make a list of the information you can give new pupils. Make it different from the instructions and advice that teachers and parents will give them.

  Here are some ideas to get you started:
  The best ways of getting to school
  Making sure your bike is safe
  What happens to bags at lunchtime
  The best dinners
  How you do homework

- On your own, use Lisa's letter and the list your group has made to write an information sheet for new pupils.

  Before you start writing, choose what you think are the five (or more) most important things that need explaining. Then, think about the clearest way of presenting your information sheet.

  Here are two different ways you might present it:
  1 Write down the questions a new pupil might ask, following each question by a direct answer explaining your advice.
  2 Write short, clear sections with headings.

  Think about the style you want to use: chatty and personal; or more factual.

  You can use maps, lists, diagrams, drawings to help communicate the information.

TASK 4 *The "inside" story* Yr 8

Aim To write about the 'things that teachers won't tell you about your new school'

- In pairs, each make a list of the things about school life that pupils know about but teachers don't. Then compare your lists and share them with other pairs.

- Read Philip's *Excuses for gullible teachers*, Matthew's *All you need to know when you're late for school* and Eric Finney's *Progress Report* (Sheets 64 and 65). Which of them do you think is the most entertaining? Explain why.

- On your own, choose two or three things to write about from your list. Then, try to think of an entertaining way to present your ideas. Here are some suggestions:

  ☐ *a short script you could write with your neighbour*
  ☐ *find out facts and opinions through a survey and present your findings*
  ☐ *a 4 or 6 frame comic strip*
  ☐ *diary entries*
  ☐ *a newspaper article*
  ☐ *an interview you write up*
  ☐ *a TV commercial story board*
  ☐ *poems or riddles*
  ☐ *drawings or photographs with captions*

  As you draft your writing, be prepared to experiment until you find the most interesting way of conveying your ideas.

The 'inside' story

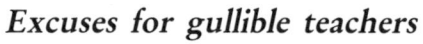

Excuses for gullible teachers

Sorry sir, I'm late.
But some Martians came down from Mars and ate
My dinner money and my pen.
But as I was running home again
To get something else with which I could write
A fire-breathing dragon set my bag alight.
So I sprinted home as fast as I could,
When a big blue pig all covered in mud
Started eating my tie, so I pushed him off
But some mud flew into my mouth and I started to cough
Once I was home I got my things and was here for half past ten.
The teacher said, 'I'll let you off, but don't let it happen again.'

Philip

All you need to know when you're late for school

Say to the teacher:
- I heard on the radio that the school had burnt down in the middle of the night.
- Someone took the stepladders from my bunk in the middle of the night.
- My dad couldn't find the key to the back door so we had to ring my uncle in Manchester to bring the spare key.
- The bus driver was new so he took the wrong turning and we ended up in Cornwall so I had to walk back.
- The cupboard fell on my mum and I needed to get it off to win my Blue Peter badge.

Matthew

The 'inside' story

Progress report

'...and you can't go
In that scruffy jacket either –
You'll look a proper fool.'
Mum and Dad getting ready to go
To the Progress Meeting
At school.
Dad says, 'Come to that,
Is that the dress you're going to wear?
Lean forward with that neckline
And your bellybutton's bare!'
They did get gone eventually,
Both suitably dressed in black,
Gone to a big session of talk
About me –
Behind my blooming back.

'He's really had an excellent term.
The work's been very demanding –
But in English, Maths, History, Geog...
In everything he's outstanding.
On the sports field too he's broken records –
Well, look at the trophies he's lifted...
And in Music he just plays everything,
He's really wonderfully gifted.'
'No weaknesses anywhere at all!' gasps Dad.
(Mum's looking over the moon).
'Absolutely none,' Sir firmly states,
'I'm sure he'll be Head Boy soon.
And meeting you both this evening,
Well, it's not difficult to see
Where your son's brilliance comes from...'
Says Mum (and Dad), 'From me!'

And that's where the dreaming ended.
'You've been asleep by the telly,' says Mum;
They were back from the Progress Meeting,
Both looking pretty glum.
'I had a bit of a dream...' I said.
'That's your problem,' said Dad,
'Dreaming instead of doing,
You need to shape yourself, my lad.
Your teacher says in English and Maths
Your marks are very low,
And in Geography, History and all that stuff –
Well, you just don't want to know.
No interest in Games or Music,' he says,
'None in Art or Drama –'
'Save the rest for the morning,' says Mum,
'By then you'll be feeling calmer.'

And I trailed off to bed
Heart heavy as lead,
Mind silently screaming,
'Better pack in the dreaming.'

Eric Finney

TASK 5 *Writing up the booklet*

Aim To collect together the different pieces of writing you have done and to present them in a booklet

- In groups, collect all the pieces of writing you have done during this assignment and select from them to put together a booklet for pupils who will be coming to your school. Think about the design of the booklet. Can you use a word processor to make a booklet with an interesting design?

  1 Choose the pieces of writing which you think will work best in the booklet and decide on the order in which you are going to place them. You'll need to think about balance and variety: a mix of pieces which are informative, amusing, the use of maps and diagrams, etc.

  2 Prepare an index or contents list.

  3 Write an introduction for the booklet or write a letter, like the one below, explaining why you have put this booklet together.

  > Dear Fourth Year reader,
  >
  > At the end of the Summer term you will no longer be a Fourth Year pupil, you will have become a newcomer in the First Year at our school. I know that you will be very nervous but there is nothing to be worried about.
  >
  > You will probably have heard lots of rumours about the school. They are not true. This is a happy school, but if you do happen to have any problems don't be scared to tell your tutor, I'm sure you'll be helped.
  >
  > I hope you have a good time at our school.
  >
  > Good luck,
  >
  > Rachel

  4 Design a cover which gives the reader an idea of the aim and contents of the booklet.

- When you have finished, show each other the booklets which you have produced. Decide whose booklet is most successful and agree on a list of points – the main features of a good booklet.

RECORDING AND ASSESSMENT

It is important that throughout the English programme students should be involved in the process of continuous self-assessment, reflecting on how successfully they have fulfilled the aims of the assignments and tasks they have completed. The teacher's expertise in drawing attention to a student's successes and assisting him/her in setting targets for future development, through written comments and discussions, will be informed by detailed knowledge of the attainment targets and the levels achieved. However, it is the dialogue between teacher and student that enables learning to take place and progress to be made, rather than time spent on recording achievements in relation to each separate attainment target on a complex grid.

The proposed system of recording and assessment, therefore, eschews complicated checklists, offering instead a review and assessment sheet to be used, as appropriate, after the completion of an assignment or a number of assignments. The spaces for student comment and teacher comment offer opportunities for summative statements, detailing the progress made in relation to the aims of the assignments which have been completed,

thus providing both an extension of the dialogue between teacher and student and a record of the student's achievement. Although the space for the student's comment is placed before that for the teacher's comment, the order in which the comments are completed could vary, depending on whether the teacher wishes to respond to the student's comments.

At the bottom of the sheet are numbered boxes for the teacher to record the student's levels of achievement in the attainment targets: speaking and listening, reading and writing. Each attainment target should be assessed holistically rather than by attempting an assessment of individual statements or strands. Experience has shown that, while a sharper focus on the different elements within each attainment target can be extremely useful, there is nothing to be gained by attempting a detailed assessment of each separate statement.

Nevertheless, it is often helpful, when assessing students' levels, to be able to refer to the separate elements within each attainment target. Sheets showing the different elements of the attainment targets for levels 3–8 are included in the Teacher's Guide.

REVIEW AND ASSESSMENT SHEET

Student's name   Date

Assignment(s) completed

Student's comments

Teacher's comments

ATTAINMENT TARGETS – Levels achieved, ring as appropriate

Speaking and listening		3	4	5	6	7	8	
Reading		3	4	5	6	7	8	
Writing		3	4	5	6	7	8	

● ●

TALKING AND WRITING FROM EXPERIENCE: RELATED STATEMENTS OF ATTAINMENT

Reading and responding to personal writing
and
Demonstrating an understanding of the content and form of a range of texts

level

3
- to demonstrate that they can find and appreciate meanings beyond the literal

4
- to demonstrate a developing ability to use inference, deduction and previous reading experience

5
- to demonstrate an ability to support their own views by reference to some details in the text

6
- to demonstrate that they are developing insights which they can sustain by reference to the text

7
- to give evidence of personal response and show an understanding of the author's approach

8
- to give evidence of personal response and show an understanding of the devices and structures writers use to achieve their effects

Talking about personal experiences
and
Demonstrating an ability to describe personal experiences and express personal viewpoints and to listen and respond to those of others

level

3-8
- to contribute to and respond constructively in group discussions

3
- to relate real events in a connected narrative

4
- to give a detailed oral account of an event

5
- to give a well organised and sustained account of an event, a personal experience or an activity
- to use language to convey information and ideas effectively in a straightforward situation

6
- to use language to convey information and ideas effectively in a variety of situations where the subject is familiar to the audience

7
- to express a personal opinion or belief clearly and cogently to a range of audiences and interpret accurately a range of statements by others
- to use and understand language which conveys information and ideas effectively to an audience which is unfamiliar with the topic

8
- to express points of view on complex matters clearly and cogently and interpret points of view with accuracy and discrimination

Writing

and

Demonstrating an ability to draft, edit and present personal writing in a variety of forms for a range of audiences and purposes

level

3
- to produce independently a range of chronological and non-chronological writing
- to begin to revise and redraft in discussion with the teacher, other adults or other children in the class

4
- to produce a range of chronological and non-chronological writing for different purposes, showing a developing ability to structure the writing in ways that make the meaning clear to the reader
- to attempt independent redrafting and revision of their writing and to talk about changes they have made

5
- to write in a variety of forms for a range of purposes and audiences in ways which attempt to engage the interest of the reader
- to produce writing in which the meaning is made clear to the reader and organisational devices and sentence punctuation are generally accurately used
- to assemble ideas on paper, or on a computer screen, or in a discussion with others, and show some ability to produce a draft from them and then to redraft and revise as necessary

6
- to write in a variety of forms for a range of purposes, presenting subject matter differently to suit the needs of specified known audiences, demonstrating the ability to sustain the interest of the reader
- to produce writing in which the subject matter is set out clearly and appropriately
- to recognise when redrafting and revising are appropriate and act accordingly, either on paper or on a computer screen

7
- to write in a wide variety of forms with commitment and a clear sense of purpose and awareness of audience, producing well-structured pieces of writing and demonstrating an ability to anticipate the reader's response
- to demonstrate an increased awareness that a first draft may be changed, amended and re-ordered in a variety of ways

8
- to write in a variety of forms with a clear sense of purpose and audience, sustaining the interest of the reader and demonstrating an assured and selective use of a wide range of grammatical constructions